THE SHADOW OF WORDS

The place that **Ana Blandiana**, pen name of Otilia Valeria Coman (*b.* Timişoara, 1942), occupies in the literary life of Romania is comparable to that of Anna Akhmatova in Russia or Václav Havel in the Czech Republic. A poet, novelist and essayist, she holds the record of three bans on her writing (1959-64, 1985, 1988-89), the first at the age of 17. Her daring, outspoken poems, along with her courageous attitude in defence of ethical values, have made her a legend in Romanian literature. She was co-founder and President of the Civic Alliance from 1990, an independent non-political organisation that fought for freedom and democratic change. She also re-founded and became President of the Romanian PEN Club; and in 1993, under the aegis of the European Community, she created the Memorial for the Victims of Communism in Sighet. In recognition of her contribution to European culture and her fight for human rights over many years, Blandiana was awarded the highest distinction of the French Republic, the Légion d'Honneur (2009), and Romanian Women of Courage Award (2014) of the US State Department. Among her numerous international literary awards, she holds the Gottfried von Herder Prize (University of Vienna, 1982), the European Poet of Freedom Prize (Gdansk, 2016), the Griffin Poetry Foundation's Lifetime Recognition Award (Toronto, 2018), the Golden Wreath Award (Academy of Arts and Sciences of North Macedonia, 2019), and the Princess Asturias Award for Letters 2024 (Oviedo). In 2021, Blandiana's novel *The Drawer with Applause* was a finalist for the Strega European Prize, following its translation into Italian.

Bloodaxe has published all of Blandiana's poetry to date in the translation of Paul Scott Derrick and Viorica Patea: *My Native Land A4* (2010), *The Sun of Hereafter / Ebb of the Senses* (2017), combining her two previous collections, which was a Poetry Book Society Recommended Translation. Two further compilations cover her other poetry collections: *Five Books* (2021), and *The Shadow of Words* (2025).

Ana Blandiana

THE SHADOW
OF WORDS

TRANSLATED BY
PAUL SCOTT DERRICK & VIORICA PATEA

BLOODAXE BOOKS

Poems copyright © Ana Blandiana 1964, 1966, 1969, 1974 1977, 1981, 2025
Translations © Paul Scott Derrick & Viorica Patea 2025

ISBN: 978 1 78037 540 3

First published 2025 by
Bloodaxe Books Ltd,
Eastburn,
South Park,
Hexham,
Northumberland NE46 1BS.

www.bloodaxebooks.com
For further information about Bloodaxe titles
please visit our website or write to
the above address for a catalogue.

Supported by
**ARTS COUNCIL
ENGLAND**

The publication of this book was supported by a grant
from the Romanian Cultural Institute, Bucharest.

INSTITUTUL
CULTURAL
R O M Â N

Cover design: Neil Astley & Pamela Robertson-Pearce.

Printed in Great Britain by Bell & Bain Limited, Glasgow, Scotland, on
acid-free paper sourced from mills with FSC chain of custody certification.

CONTENTS

THE THIRD SACRAMENT (1969)

SLEEP WITHIN SLEEP (1977)

INTRODUCTION

The Quest for the Shadow of Words

The four books of Ana Blandiana's early poems in this collection appeared from 1964 to 1981, the first three during the brief period of political thaw of the communist regime (1964-1971), when aestheticism took on a subversive role, reaffirming the autonomy of the poetic word. In these poems, Blandiana reveals herself as a poet both of the intimate and of the life of the *polis*, or as the German theologian Dietrich Bonhoeffer would say, a writer who combines 'the joy of a hidden life and the courage for public life'. As in T.S. Eliot's poetry, sensual perception and intellectual analysis merge. In a voice articulating a vibrant spiritual language of unmistakable ethical clarity, Blandiana's poems call for moral regeneration in the face of indifference. Their pure idealism overrides the many masks of degradation. These youthful lyrics announce from the outset the sense of responsibility and faith in the survival of the collective soul that has characterised Blandiana's poetry ever since.

The Drama of 'Dying in White': East-Aesthetics of Purity in the Early Poems of Ana Blandiana. *First Person Plural* (1964) and *Achilles' Heel* (1966)

After being banned at age 17 for publishing a poem in the Transylvanian magazine, *Tribuna*, Blandiana made her debut in 1964 with a first collection that would bear the premonitory title, *First Person Plural*, published in a period of political thaw (1964-1971). Although this era of relative liberalism was short-lived, it nevertheless put an end to almost two decades of 'socialist realism' or *proletcult*, imposed by Moscow on all countries behind the Iron Curtain. The brief lull in the political climate allowed a generation of Romanian poets to explore new forms of expression. The poets of the 60s Generation, to which Blandiana belongs, recovered the

Orphic, confessional, intimate and sometimes metaphysical tone of poetry, initiating a dialogue with the great avant-garde tradition of the interwar period and invoking memory of a free world, interrupted by the establishment of the communist regime.

While aestheticism is generally associated with the doctrine of 'art for art's sake' of such writers as Victor Cousin, Benjamin Constant and Edgar Allan Poe, or the 'pure poetry' of Mallarmé, with its apparent evasion of reality and retreat to the poet's ivory tower, in East European countries, aesthetics acquired a subversive role, to the extent that it rejected official propaganda. In *First Person Plural*, Blandiana intones a hymn to the courage of her generation: 'Who would ever dare to offend / My generation's epaulettes?' ('Pride'). She is proud of this group of poets who have never knelt. And she openly attributes the boldness and audacity she discovers in herself to her fellow poets: 'My eyes have never glanced towards the earth. / My ankles have never been gripped by a chain' ('Dance in the Rain').

More importantly, *First Person Plural* foreshadows Blandiana's subsequent trajectory as a poet who embraces poetry as her destiny. The title itself expresses the desire of the poet to define herself in conjunction with the world. Her poems describe the frenzy of living in harmony with nature's rhythms in poems that celebrate life with an effervescent energy. The self is surrounded by a bounty of natural colours and sounds compelling an urgency to live. In 'Rain Chant', for instance, while the wind moulds the speaker's body around her dress, she resembles a winged Victoria of Samothrace, messenger of femininity and endless vitality:

> I love the rain, I love the rain with passion,
> The madcap rain, the quiet rain,
> The virginal rain and the rain like a hot-blooded woman.

Although *First Person Plural* shimmers with the lyricism of being's purity and fragility, as well as with astonishment at life, it nevertheless contains poems of gloom and melancholy, too. Hopeful and confident in their destiny, the young people Blandiana portrays return to a 'sad' city dragging 'the dead / Cat of the mists' ('Victors'). Two years later, *Achilles' Heel* (1966) intensified these pockets of gloom with more radical poetic language. With her earlier purity confronted by registers of deterioration, the poet's beleaguered sensibility commits her to struggle against the degradation of existence, both physical and moral, in an era in which the falsification of truth proliferates everywhere.

Sensual exaltation gives way to profound meditative moods. Where the protagonist in *First Person Plural* adopts the pose of a self-assured adolescent, who allows herself to be embraced by the sweeping rains as she discovers the miracle of existence, in *Achilles' Heel* her universe is shaken by turmoil: Snow gives birth to worms ('Drawing in Pastel'), dirty light flows through canals ('Flow'), and the world's foundations seem threatened by the corruption inherent in silence. Voyages are not real, 'Cruises' set sail to 'Almost-real departures into the world', and people do not go anywhere but embark on ships that remain 'moored to the port', watched by 'the watchful, fatherly eye of the lighthouse / At our backs', alluding to the secret police who condemn them to 'non-adventure'. In this world without freedom explorations are fictitious: 'fish never seen before, / With plants of unknown colours' mark a fissure in reality ('Cruises'). Blandiana's earlier frenzied lyricism of hope for an ethical ideal is replaced by anguish and uncertainty, permeated by a diffuse sense of guilt. The lyrical self discovers that the universe is governed by unjust laws, whose degradation is not only temporary or physical, but soon infects other values, such as gratitude, degenerating into the mere calculation of reward ('The Change on the Table'). In this fluctuating, liquid world, the poet desperately seeks '[t]he fulcrum of the universe' ('The Return'), an ideal ethical territory nowhere to be found except in her own conscience.

The phenomenon of degradation is an unavoidable aspect of existence whose *raison d'être* is precisely the negation of purity:

> I know that purity yields no fruit,
> That virgins don't give birth,
> And the great law of defilement
> Is the tribute to life on earth.
>
> ('I Know That Purity')

These lines recall Sylvia Plath's lines, 'Perfection is terrible / It cannot have children' ('The Munich Mannequins', 1963). The great dilemma of the self is either 'dying in white' or submitting to 'the great law of defilement'. Lost between 'silence and / Sin', she knows not whether to persist in the realm of purity, which is that of no life, or to debase herself under the law of life, which her sense of dignity rejects.

In this context, for Blandiana poetry becomes a curse that transforms things into words and camouflages the authenticity of life. 'The gift' of poetry becomes 'tragic'; as in antiquity, it is a 'curse' the poet must atone for. Everything the poet touches 'Turns to words, just as in the myth of Midas' ('The Gift'). For the lyric self, no suffering is greater than not being able to separate things from the deforming veil of words. In 'Quarantine', a poem on the death of her father, Blandiana expresses her distrust of the word ('Oh Lord, how much literature we contain!'), as well as the possibility of overcoming the barriers that separate us from the other: 'Pain is not contagious, it separates / Us more effectively than walls.' Words prove incapable of overcoming the insurmountable loneliness of the self, especially in the face of death: 'They all shed tears around the dying man's bed, / But no one is contaminated with death.'

The duty of poets is to stop this process of degradation. That is why Blandiana adopts an aesthetic of clear colours, of forms without equivocation or ambiguity, of inviolable values that confront the constant delusions between reality and appearance, truth and falsehood. In 'Intolerance' she declares,

I want clear tones,
I want clear words,
I want to feel the muscles of words with my hand,
I want to understand what you are, what I am,
And clearly distinguish a laugh from a curse.

As an 'adventure of being honest' ('Return'), poetry must express this ethical rigour through a geometry of pure forms and strive, as the Romanian critic Eugen Simion affirms, for 'essential colours'.[1]

---

1. Eugen Simion, 'Ana Blandiana', *Scriitori români azi*, Bucharest: Editura Cartea Românească, 1978, p. 332.

For this reason, nuances do not enrich, but adulterate reality: 'many thousands of shades rot a colour…' ('Have We Grown Up?'). Adulthood implies adapting to ambiguity, equivocation, misrepresentation, and confusion. Achilles' vulnerable heel, invoked in the volume's title, points to this zone of a redeeming candour on which 'the fate of the whole universe' depends to halt the disintegrating impact of time on the self.

To define the poet's role, Blandiana re-writes myth, as when in 'Where Is the Pride?' she asserts how, like Orpheus, a poet will have to soften the wild beasts yet at the same time be Eurydice, two roles that she adopts and reverses interchangeably. The artist's anti-model is Torquato Tasso, the Italian Renaissance poet 'spoiled by fear' whom Blandiana rejects because of the 'Poetry unwritten out of fear', since he stopped writing to protect himself from the Inquisition. Instead, she contends that poetry must defy the vicissitudes of history. Conversely, in 'Of Austerity and Naïveté', the last poem in the book, she looks to the exemplary figure of Racine, the French neoclassical playwright who wrote *Phaedra*. As a young man, Racine abandoned the Jansenist austerity of the monastery of Port-Royal where he had been educated to pursue glory and fame at the royal court – 'Phèdre awaits me, and the king'–, although in time he came to lament having given up the monastic life governed by ethical rigour.

To counter time's devastating effects, Blandiana proposes reversing chronology, so that moving forward is not a departure from our beginnings, but a return to primordial innocence. The poem 'We Should Be' attempts to save purity by inverting time in the seven ages of man. 'We Should Be Born Old', the poet insists, so that at the end of our lives we regress to the seed stage. In this way, our vital trajectory advances against the clock towards the innocence of *illo tempore*.

Given that poetry is a fundamental choice, by accepting her destiny as a poet, the 'I' renounces 'The happy common slumber' ('Where is the pride?') for the struggle with the inertia of others and, in particular, with the 'great silence' of those dwelling in 'shells' who 'artistically mould their silence into shields: / Wisdom-silence, contempt-silence' ('In Great Silence').

However, such ethical determination sets up an irreconcilable clash between innocence and degradation. In 'Morning Elegy', the poet assumes the role of a new redeemer who comes to save humanity through her sacrifice. She does not bring fire, like Prometheus, but snow: 'I snowed on the city all night for you, / I made the dark night white for you.' She announces a new religion of snow, a pristine purity sent to overcome the hypocrisy, conformism and lies of the world.[2] Here the lyrical self takes the form of a demiurge who snows, absolving a universe sullied by ash, 'the dust of the mortal fire', which people routinely sow in the morning 'like wheat'. Snow here can redeem all earthly defilement, as this Prometheus of the snows becomes prophetic, bequeathing a crusade of the snows, an avalanche of cosmic proportions, a kind of white purgatory to establish a new order in which 'whiteness will cover your weak denial' and 'like a burning sun of snow', the good will prevail.

Indeed, white is Blandiana's favourite colour, and she will take up the motif of snow in more detail in her later volume, *Sleep within Sleep*, where poems such as 'Prayer', 'When I Wake Up' and 'The Morning after Death' project the resurrection in a white, pure and spiritualised world, where the snow promises a regenerated humanity. Snow, 'White with no edges / And peace with no beginning,' is invoked to restore innocence to the world.

The Metaphysical Elegy of Being: *The Third Sacrament* (1969)

Published when Blandiana was 27, *A treia taină* (*The Third Sacrament*, 1969) demonstrates proof of a maturity beyond the poet's age. In Romanian, the term '*taină*' encompasses a range of meanings, including 'mystery', 'secret', and 'enigma'. Furthermore, the term is used to denote the seven sacraments, the third of which is the Eucharist, the distinctive symbol of spirituality and Christianity. The sacramental consecration represents the pinnacle of unity

---

2. Viorel Chirilă,'Purgatoriul zăpezii', *Familia*, n.° 3, 1992, pp. 4-5.

among humanity, the divine, the natural world and the Word. The Eucharist represents the archetypal divine through which created entities participate in a supernatural relationship which affirms the unity of the material and the spiritual of all four elements and exemplifies the manifestation of God's presence in the world. Under this doctrine, nature and human history may be regarded as exemplars of the divine, as the Eucharist serves as a conduit for love, sanctification, communion, and unity in Christ. Through this sacrament, individuals accept Christ's sacrifice and redemption.

Conversely, poetry can be considered a form of mystery, in the original sense of the term, encompassing such concepts as sacrament, communion and confession. Similarly, *The Third Sacrament* (1969) can be read as a confession in which personal experience is imbued with metaphysical significance. This volume comprises a selection of Blandiana's most notable poems, in which her language is ascetic yet disturbing, austere yet hieratic, in poetry that tends towards the paradoxical in figurative language that almost reaches transparency. Throughout the collection the idea of transubstantiation and love prevails. In addition to her earlier ethical and social considerations, Blandiana now explores existential aspects of the self's place in the world. The desire for the absolute and for purity engulfs the self, who, weary of moral asceticism, seeks solace in sleep and returns to the organic, seeking integration with cosmic rhythms. Poetry evinces a nostalgia for the uncreated and primordial. But an additional central theme is the thirst for knowledge. The 'I' follows the flight of a 'Bird' that appears to possess knowledge of the great mysteries on its way to an unknown destination. However, the bird's flight accelerates rapidly, and its message is obscured by peripheral noise. Still, the persona further implores the elders to disclose the 'terrible mystery' of existence which they possess ('You Know Something').

A book characterised by a pervasive sense of melancholy,[3] *The Third Sacrament* follows Blandiana's previous volumes in displaying a notable degree of candour and sincerity. She increasingly and

---

3. Constantin Ciopraga, 'Cinci poeți', *România Literară*, year xvii, no 32, Thursday August 9, 1984, p. 4-5.

persistently examines the fundamental mysteries of life, love, the nature of the self and its place within the expanse of the universe. In the face of glaring incongruities between the conceptual ideal and a reality indifferent to ethical principles, the lyrical 'I' laments its helplessness to alter the world while simultaneously acknowledging a sense of guilt for accepting the world's limited condition, even when favourable:

> I can't stop the day from lasting twenty-four hours.
> I can only say:
> Forgive me for the length of the day.
> I can't stop silkworms from turning into butterflies.
> I can only ask you to forgive me
> For the silkworm, for the butterfly.
> Forgive me if flowers turn into fruit
> The fruit into seeds, the seeds into trees.
> Forgive me if springs turn into rivers,
> Rivers into seas, seas into oceans.
> Forgive me if love turns into new-born babies,
> New-born babies into loneliness, and loneliness into love…
> No. I can't stop anything.
> Everything follows its course.
> Nothing consults with me –
> Not the last grain of sand, not even my blood.
> I can only ask you to
> Forgive me.

> ('Humility')

Blandiana's vision here is predicated on tenets of panpsychism, which postulates that all entities are imbued with a universal mind endowed with psychic attributes. The universe can be conceived as an infinite projection of the self, as a multiplicity of faces pursuing and reflecting it. In order to affirm her own identity, the poetic persona must rediscover the enigmatic connections with the universe that bear her imprint: 'Show me a leaf that doesn't look like me, / Help me to find an animal / That doesn't moan with my voice.' ('Ties'). However, this projection also has the qualities of an aggressor, a double who challenges the self; therefore, she avows: 'my only defence is to lash out against myself'. The idea that 'Everything is me' posits an analogy of the self as the world, suggesting an indissoluble unity that transcends even death. 'And I see how the dead, who have my face,' she concludes, 'Embrace and give birth to more and more dead' ('Ties').

As in her earlier poems, time cannot be understood without its fusion with the self, as when she compares herself to 'sand in an hourglass / that can / only / be time / when / it falls' ('Condition'). Time passing continues to have the effect of emptying the self and altering it. The past modifies the present, leaving the self unable to discern traces of actions in the world: 'I look at the past and I don't understand / The footprints I've left behind' only the signs of a forgotten language remain, but their meanings have been lost, 'signs / In the alphabet of a vanished language' ('Contretemps').

In a universe subject to a blind determinism or implacable randomness ruled by forces of mutual annihilation, the poet's primary focus is to understand the boundaries between good and evil. The self simply cannot discern the unstable, yet ubiquitous frontier that separates these ethical antinomies, which, on the other hand, underscore the paradoxical nature of mystery. Furthermore, the difficulty of discerning opposites is only compounded by the indissoluble unity between them. In effect, God and Satan sit at the two ends of the same seesaw, so for God to be always 'On the side of the board / Lifted into the air' ('Alternative'), he needs a counterweight. Satan is the *sine qua non* principle, without which God could not exist. What is more: good produces the evil with which it is punished. In 'Everything Simple', 'all the terrible shadows' cast by the candle would not exist, were it not for the evil that 'light has brought into the world…'. There are no cardinal points indicating the absolute, no guiding principle, no 'north' or 'line between good and evil', since 'evil always stops before / I can find the border' ('Borderline'). In 'The North' none of us can 'know / Who we are, and how. / Behind us, a line of unknown parents, / Before us, a line of unknown sons'. Searching for the frontier that separates good from evil, Blandiana discovers instead the sheer impossibility of capturing the mysteries of 'On this earth / That's sometimes cloudy, / Sometimes sunny' ('The Frontier'). 'No answer is born,' she states unequivocally in 'Contretemps', adding ghoulishly, 'Except when no one needs it / Any more / And the question that awaited it / Has died.'

Regardless, the poems in *The Third Sacrament* give voice to an alert conscience that rejects the conventional dictates of obedience and accepted truths. 'By Our Own Will' refers to how we freely submit to censorship. This acceptance of prohibitions – evident in 'An incomplete gesture, a smile bitten off, / And what a disaster of beloved corpses we have now –/ By our own will, by our own will, by our own will / Forbidden, punished, repressed' – reveals an attitude that expels the self from natural order, so that the persona loses her fluid relationship with the world. Trees, water and animals shy away from her, as 'the universe, horrified, sees in me / A kind of submission it didn't engender'. In 'Psalm', the wisdom of prudence – or what 'They taught me not to say' – disrupts natural harmony and breaches faith: 'The cranes betray, the trees surrender.' Losing an organic relationship with the universe results in alienation: 'I walk around inside myself / Like I'd wander through a foreign city / Where I don't know a single soul' ('Journey'). The poet feels estranged even from her own name, in which she no longer recognises herself ('Far away').

Self-censorship, or refusing to act in the face of injustice, turns us into 'docile witnesses to the crime…', whom the poet exhorts, 'While we still have time' to 'hide the living words' ('While We Still Have Time'). Whether from common usage or ideological manipulation, words are altered and degraded. Stereotyped, they lose their vitality and 'fresh words' are replaced by 'dead words'. Blandiana describes this process ironically as a recipe: 'Take fresh words and pronounce them / Until uniform and polished / And no one remembers / What form and meaning they had before' ('While We Still Have Time'). Meanwhile, the dead words iterate the living dead, the 'docile dead', who 'let themselves be harnessed in banners' and whose 'gestures sculpted by others' are subject to a servile patriotism ('Fatigue'). The poet's obsessive care to rescue those same 'living words' from falsification ultimately is an attempt to rescue poetry itself. To save the Logos, she must extract 'the sacred bone', that which conceptually designates their meaning or 'shadow'.

In fact, in *Fifty Poems* (1970), a volume comprised of a further ten poems from Blandiana's poetic anthology included here, words take on a second life, with a destiny in and beyond death:

> Let the words fall
> Just like the fruits, just like the leaves,
> Only those in which death has matured.
> Let's drop them
> Almost rotten,
> Barely wearing on their flesh
> The sacred bone.
> The open hollow bone,
> As from the withered clouds the moon,
> Perhaps, he will secretly descend to earth…
>
> ('Let the Words Fall')

Throughout *The Third Sacrament*, Blandiana's visionary imagination construes a mythical framework with strong Platonic accents. She offers ingenious versions of known myths which she often rewrites in the guise of humorous children's games. The poet foresees the moment of reincarnation. In the book's first poem, the soul must choose what form it will take in its future life. But neither 'man, nor woman, / Nor animal I wanted to be, / Nor bird, nor plant'. The lyric voice feels that any choice is a limitation. Individualisation inevitably requires fragmentation from the great whole, so the poet makes 'No Choice'. The soul refuses to take on any form, since all of them are limited ('Indecision').

In similar fashion, a recurrent motif throughout Blandiana's poetry is the descent of the sacred into the existential, in a universe where sin is replaced by the idea of the devitalisation of heaven. Angels do not fall 'because of sin, / But because they're just worn out', weary of eternity. Elsewhere 'The prophets died out in the desert' and angels 'dragging their wings on the ground, / Were placed in rows in the squares. / Soon they'll be tried' ('The Fall'). Blandiana's worldview here is fundamentally Platonic, constructing an imaginary world that lacks intrinsic consistency: 'I don't dare to close my eyes for an instant. / I'm afraid / I'll crush the world between my lids' ('Eye-Blink'). The universe itself is perceived as a 'docile Animal', its 'Planets circulating / Like red and white blood cells', while 'We are its eyes, / Which he opened late / Like the eyes of a cat', eyes that 'can do nothing / But see' ('The Docile Animal'). Such reconstructed myths proliferate in Blandiana's poetry, at once distressing but invigorating.

Blandiana's universe is also rooted in love, as 'Something indes- tructible' [that] 'Flows between parents and children'. Yet the quasi- religious metaphor of such sentiment is always linked to suffering, guilt and death: 'Only the love between parents and children / Is seed,' she writes in 'Only Love', though Love is above 'the laws of this world', since it is 'a holy sacrament'. 'The entire universe is hanging / From this thread of blood that joins us,' she declares ('Only Love'). This love is defined under three fundamental aspects: father, beloved, and son, all belonging to the same affective spectrum: 'You are my son, my love, / Everything stems from that. /.../ / Come close to me, like a child, / And kiss me, father, on the lips' ('Only Love').

In 'Requiem'– a poem linked to the tragic death of Blandiana's father – the search for origins is associated with the archetypal paternal figure: 'My naive father, / The tragic Gheorghe'. In 'Pietà', the filial sentiment imbued with religiosity gives rise to the sacred nature of maternal love. The poem recreates the biblical scene of Christ's descent from the cross, featuring the key figures of the son, the mother, the cross, the disciples, and the father, who is 'intuited, not spoken of'. Cradling her son in secret, the sorrowful mother represents the epitome of maternal love, while the son, longing to 'rest / In death and in [her] lap' epitomises filial affection. Her metaphysical restlessness alternates with her son's desire to remain in the transitory, attempting to postpone the return to eternity:

> Three days only
> But until then
> I feel so good
> In your lap, brought down from the cross,
> And, if I didn't fear to frighten you,
> I would turn my mouth
> To your breast, and suckle.

Love here mediates between the human and the divine.[4] The self represents the locus of divine love, encompassing both the transcendent descending into the self and the latter's aspiration to the divine. As Iulian Boldea notes, the drama of Christ here epitomises the tragic sentiment

> through an alternation between the concrete and the transcendent whereby suffering acquires a metaphysical aura without losing its human attributes. The body and the sacrament are ambivalent poetic expressions. The expressed and the unexpressed intertwine to create a lyrical picture... [reaching] a transparency that enhances the experience of the sacred. The sentiment of filial piety, comprising elements of religiosity, suffering, guilt and death, is conveyed as a lament. This evokes a gravity that transcends the clay and elevates the vision to metaphysical dimensions.[5]

Additionally, the poems in *Fifty Poems* share a common theme and atmosphere, with the dominant element being autumn and the gradual decline of nature. Figuratively, here the self is revealed to be fragile, on the threshold of death, as these poems portray an attempt to reconcile the self and the universe, the human and the transcendent. In the words of Eugen Simion, through the symbols of the sacred figuration (God, the Son) and the metaphor of the end, *Fifty Poems* (1970) articulate a 'metaphysical elegy'.[6] The poems comprise a monologue addressed to the other, who is the divinity. They express anguish in the face of death and a keen sense of the presence of the numinous. The persona, who sees herself as having 'never been more mortal' ('Death in Light' #6), explores the relationship of the transient and the eternal. The dead soul meets the soul of the living in 'A spear of grass' ('Encounter'), 'Night is falling above the calendars', and 'naked souls, [are] dying in the grass' ('The Soul'). In the premonitory stillness of autumn, tears

---

4. Codruța Oana Bușu, *Ana Blandiana. Studiu monografic*, Craiova: Editura Sitech, 2010, p. 95.
5. Iulian Boldea, *Ana Blandiana. Monografie, antologie comentată, receptare critică*, Brașov: Editura Aula, 2000, p. 86.
6. Eugen Simion, 'Prefață', *Poezii*, București: Editura BPT, p. xiii.

drip from the sky ('October'), while the poet yearns for the wind of non-being, turns to her beloved, whom night resurrects, and turns him into her brother, only to become again her father.

'Up there' 'on the mountain', the house that appears and disappears, like the moon among the clouds, is the abode of the soul, a symbol of faith and the transcendent, perhaps a memory of the past or a premonition: 'Do we remember it from another life / Or is it only a horrible foreboding?' The allure of the enigma compels us to remain suspended 'from that humid icon like / Tears in the lashes of gods unnamed', pondering the creator as a simultaneously transcendent and immanent presence. The autumn rain in the form of 'Warm tears' which drip 'Softly / Onto my eyelids', is a metaphor of the 'father' who in the act of weeping 'adopts' her

> Who is crying above me
> And turning
> His sweet tears
> Into mine,
> Father
> Or maybe a stranger
> Who adopts me this way?

> ('October')

Blandiana embodies religious feelings in a poetic expression grounded in intuition and the experience of the mystery. The 'Pietà', symbolic of faith, is recast in an original vision of love and the motif of Christ's descent from the cross. This biblical stamp is less pronounced in *Fifty Poems* than in *Sleep within Sleep* where the former exhibits a more personal symbolism, though closely aligned with the esoteric embedded in the sacred texts. It would be inaccurate to describe these lyrics as religious poetry; rather, the poems in *Fifty Poems* encapsulate the experience of the mystery.

Overall, *The Third Sacrament* signals the recurrence of significant themes in Blandiana's subsequent works. From this volume onwards, Blandiana's work focuses on exploring the unknowable mystery, not to unravel it, but rather to protect and preserve it as a manifestation of beauty. The poet portrays herself as one whose work is informed by an intuitive sense of mystery engaged in the depths of being. In this volume, Blandiana achieves a distinctive voice and mark of personal identity.

The Metaphysics of Sleep and the Boycott of History. *Sleep within Sleep* (1977)

Poems (1974) and *Sleep within Sleep* (1977) offer an intricate treatise on the multiple meanings of sleep conceived as the imagination yearning to overcome the limitations of a precarious reality until the concrete world is seen in a light that makes us question the existence of the physical world. Moreover, sleep and dreams signify antagonistic values: on the one hand, they highlight the metaphysical dimension of the real world, concealed by materialistic absolutism; on the other, they imply an escape from reality into a virtual realm rendered as a boycott of existence.

Blandiana's poetry can be read as a variation of Pedro Calderón de la Barca's adage, 'Life Is a Dream' (1635) and a new reading of the romantic Mihai Eminescu's (1850-89) aphorism in his poem, 'Emperor and Proletarian', 'As a dream of eternal death is the life of the whole world' (1874). For Blandiana, life is a dream, a dream within a dream in which the self is dreamt by another, who, in turn, exists in yet another's dream – all comprising but 'The Dream / Of a certain / Dream' ('Genealogy').These poems transport us to a labyrinthine universe where reality dissolves into the hallucinatory world of some-one who 'Is Dreaming Me', a world constructed from the ephemeral substance of the dream by a demiurge, drowsy and capricious, who determines the fluctuating forms of reality according to the vicissitudes of his own destiny ('Maybe Someone Is Dreaming Me'). Existence is but the reflection of a series of dreams that would not be possible without the awakening of 'The primal Lord / Of all sleep, / Asleep at / The foundations of the world / In a dream.' ('Genealogy').

As *Poems* (1974) and *Sleep within Sleep* unfold 'Between Worlds', the persona 'moves from one life to another', always on the border between dream and reality, life and death, in the 'Fragile land, / Delicate frontier / Of hours / Between two worlds that devour each other / In a ceaseless / Tug-of-war'. This frontier separates the pure from the impure, being from non-being, although sometimes this dividing line vanishes, and life coexists with death. Autumn, sleep and death define 'This triumphant / No-man's-land / Between life and death, / This bliss / That embraces the world' ('Who Said It Was Gold'). In dream, things acquire transparency and a mythical dimension in which gravity is transformed into flight, movements slow down, and *things* dissolve into light, revealing reality's ideal and transcendent aspects: 'Poplars and Maples' are 'The slender angels / Of a verdant paradise', and in 'The Village', 'Churches don't have roofs / But wings made of tiles folded close to / Their bodies'.

Blandiana's poetry becomes incantatory, as magic transfigures reality, while trees, grass and birds are enveloped in the aura of the fantastic. The sun, the angels, fruit, the old god, the worm, autumn, and earth exist together in a dreamlike terrain aspiring to the great dream from which the world and the self will be reborn purified by snow. Blandiana's imagery is pastoral and bucolic. In 'As Though the Moon Had Something to Say', the moon conveys messages in a forgotten language, and in the 'Early Gathered Grass' a gentle voice whispers that 'God is getting sleepy'. Dreamlike, this bucolic space induces metaphysical speculations. Charged by the mystery of life and death, Blandiana's pastel paintings are imbued with joy and melancholy together in the face of an imminent end ('Lascivious Fruit', 'I'm Drowsy').

Permeated by an ineffable geometry of correspondences and subtle symmetries, the universe has a secret order about it. The roundness of the 'Hills' is complemented by the curvature of the sky, silhouetted against the horizon. The hills belong both to earth and to heaven, to the dead buried in the ground and to the living, whose lives they endlessly prolong in their undulating movement that passes eternity on to the earth and vice versa. Their undulating forms in earth and sky, as Codruța Oana Bușu rightly observes, are complementary manifestations of spirit and matter, of the heartbeat nourished equally by Eros and Thanatos.[7]

---

7. Codruța Oana Bușu, *Ana Blandiana. Studiu monografic*, Craiova: Editura Sitech, 2010, p. 100.

Oddly, in autumn, her favourite season, Blandiana senses a higher design beyond death: 'Why do cautious flowers take shelter / In seeds and bees retreat into hives, / When the autumn is so kind and good / And teaches us how to die?' ('Why'), she asks. The poet returns to autumn with a longing to know 'the happy ordeal / Of the grape that settles into wine and dies' ('I Come Back to Autumn'). Autumn, like the dream, is 'this ultimate kingdom', the great unnameable mystery as prelude to death, for which there are no words, only a 'bliss / That embraces the world / In its vegetal light'. The golden colour of autumn in 'the ecstasy of [the] leaves' ('Who Said It Was Gold') unleashes an exuberant vitality before death, and the self yearns to orchestrate its own destiny to the organic rhythms of death and birth.

In these poems, Blandiana erases the boundaries between life and death, not to mark the end, not as annihilation, but as an agent of the transformations through which life exercises its dominion. Again and again her poems offer memorable definitions of death as a continuation of life, bringing her closer to mysticism, in which death is 'that childlike country / From which / A mysterious catastrophe / Separates us / In vain' ('I Do Not Sing the Leaf').

The *Mioritic* Space

Throughout, Blandiana enriches her motifs of the dream, the village, and the longing for serenity with a breadth derived from a long tradition in Romanian literature. She draws on the philosophy of the Romanian poet Lucian Blaga (1895-1961), who elevated the village to a philosophical category, finding in it a bastion of eternal essences. In Blandiana's lyrical version of myth, the village, to which she always returns, also configures a timeless, territory of the soul, and an enchanted repository of a country's foundational identity, comparable to Wordsworth's and Coleridge's idealistic notion of nature as bastion of eternal forms. Blandiana's 'A Village' creates a trope in which nature acquires a spirit invested with the autochthonous characteristics of the Danube-Pontic-Carpathian region ('In the Country's Soul', 'Drawing in Pastel'). She envisions the village as a cosmic horizon and interprets Romania's history in the light of the founding identity of its culture, expressed in two anonymous popular ballads, 'Miorița' and 'The Master Manole', which epitomise the Romanian people's philosophy of life.

'Miorița' tells the story of two shepherds from Transylvania and Wallachia who, out of envy, conspire to kill a shepherd from Moldavia – the three regions that comprise present Romania – in a plot to overtake his larger flock. A small, enchanted ewe informs the shepherd of their plan but, instead of trying to prevent the fatal outcome, he starts preparing for his death as a cosmic wedding, with the mountains as priests, the moon and the sun as godparents, and the trees and birds as guests. But as Dumitru Micu observes,[8] Blandiana offers a new version of the mioritic space, in which death initiates a sweet and gentle dissolution in the scent of flowers and the buzzing of bees. Her poem, 'I Think Clouds', bears the imprint of these two pastoral ballads:

> I think clouds must tell different
> Stories in different lands,
> Maybe there are places where
> People can see epics in the sky –
> In our country flocks cross over the heavenly vault
> With ageing dogs and melancholy lambs
> Followed by a trio of shepherds
> In the azure meadow.
> Or, as in a dream,
> An unearthly monastery rises
> To be shattered in the merciless chaos
> By the breath of a wind
> And to rebel in heaven again
> Until wings made of tiles
> Fly upwards in fear
> From the tears of a word.

---

8. Dumitru Micu, 'Lirism eutanasic', *Limbaje moderne în poezia românească azi*, Bucharest: Editura Minerva, 1986, pp. 253-269; 'Neo-romantism cu accente expresioniste Ana Blandiana', *Literatura română in secolul al xx-lea*, Bucharest: Editura Fundației Culturale Române, 2000, pp. 187-189.

The 'unearthly monastery' here alludes to 'The Master Manole', the story of a craftsman in charge of building a monastery which for unknown reasons collapses every night; its construction is only possible after he sacrifices the person he loves most, his wife Anne, whom he is forced to enclose within the walls of the church. After completing the sanctuary, he commits suicide by throwing himself from the top. In Blandiana's poem, however, the monastery does not fall but 'rises', illustrating how sacrifice is essential to any act of creation. Blandiana links the allegory of the monastery to national destiny and the tears from which poetry is born. The poem denounces the fatality of the history of a small country at the crossroads of three empires. The hero of this *mioritic* space is 'Avram Iancu' (1824-72), champion of the liberation of the serfs of Transylvania. Nevertheless, Blandiana considers this tragic destiny to be existentially enriching and, paradoxically, superior to that of other, more fortunate countries that enjoy 'a clear sky' without wounds or traumas, since for her, as for the existentialist Søren Kierkegaard, suffering is a spiritual heritage that enriches the individual and favours his or her salvation: 'How could we wish for / A clear sky and an empty dome above / When the clouds tell stories / That save us for eternity? / Batter us, storms / And make us flourish, pain / As long as you can write with sacred / Vapours on the ceiling of the world…' ('I Think the Clouds').

In 'Shepherd of Snow', Blandiana also rewrites the *mioritic* myth in her own key. Here instead of lambs the lyrical 'I' in the persona of a shepherd takes on large flocks of snowflakes, which, reminiscent of her earlier poems, she guides as a prophet of purity through the sky to empower their whiteness, initiating a feat of celestial trans-humance. Indeed, the act of shepherding is fundamentally inscribed in Romanian identity. Like a demiurge, she shapes each flake with her eyes, as great herds cross 'the infinite sky', becoming 'whiter than before'. The cycles of celestial transhumance take on a hallowed existence, projected across a sacred horizon. The shepherd joins in this epic of redeeming snow, as 'we'll all flow away / in immaculate, intended transmigration'. It is a common deed that unites all across time with a sanctified purpose, based on the symbolic sacrifice of the flocks: 'I'll wait until the heat of summer slays / My lambs to give the sweet earth its needed libation.'

As Al. Cistelecan notes,[9] in Blandiana's conception, purity and candour are indispensable for the awakening of the conscience to its responsibility. Like the English Romantics, Blandiana conceives of candour as a spiritual model, a guiding norm that sensitises the self to the world's mystery and at the same time constitutes a moral imperative.

The Boycott of History

The 'Sleep within Sleep' that gives this volume its title appears in two poems, 'I Only Need to Go to Sleep' and 'In My Sleep'. If, in the first poem, the dream, as 'light that suffuses into light', highlights an ideal dimension of existence, in the second, that dream becomes poisonous because it implies an escape into a virtual space where the self renounces its ethical responsibility. Sleep here stands for moral abdication, a tacit way of repression by people who dare utter the truth only in dreams:

> But wise neighbours only scream
> When they're sure
> That they dream they're asleep,
> In a sleep within sleep
> Where no one can hear them
> And they can say whatever they want.

('In My Sleep')

By speaking the truth only 'In a sleep within sleep', the 'lunatic heroes' avoid possible reprisals. They dare rebel only in their sleep, where their protests cannot be punished ('Poem'). They conceive of life as mere survival, relinquishing their freedom to take refuge in sleep, in a parable of the boycott of history. Doing so, they condemn themselves to a living death, in which 'Everyone living in the village was asleep / And might have dreamt that they didn't exist.' In Blandiana's later poems, this topos of sleep takes on negative connotations, as the historical stigma of a nation crushed by history.

9. Al. Cistelecan, 'Aproprierea de Blaga', *Poezie și livresc*, Bucharest: Cartea Românească, 1987, pp. 143-154.

The Shadow of Words:
Looking through the Eyes of a Cricket (1981)

After the earthquake of 1977, when the building in which she was living in the centre of Bucharest collapsed and her husband was buried under the rubble for several days, Blandiana moved to Comana, a small village lost in the Danube plain, taking up residence in a typical peasant adobe house with an orchard full of trees. She had always lived in an urban environment and now, at the age of 35, she discovered that 'everything natural is a miracle'. Living in the countryside meant distancing herself from the social problems of the metropolis. The spectacle of nature in constant regeneration led her to conclude that 'nature is not only one of the forms of absolute beauty, but the way to understand the link between life and death, and between generations' and that 'contemplating nature is an attempt to understand the miracle, the mystery that creates it and gives it meaning'. Tending the garden gave her 'the feeling that I am never alone, and this recognition of the miracle of nature is for me the definition of God'.[10]

The Cricket's Eye (1981) takes up the oneiric motifs already present in *Sleep within Sleep* (1977) but in a renewed vision. Candour, nostalgia for a return to nature, poetry as well as poetic creativity become her predominant themes, as Blandiana views the world from 'the eye of a cricket', the smallest and most insignificant animal, singer of summer and symbol of the poet. Like Emily Dickinson, Blandiana chooses simple, common elements to explore the depths of existence. In visionary vignettes, she is astonished by 'the tiny chalice of the flower', and its 'deep and vibrating / Sound like the moan of a cathedral', as she wonders 'For whom do the bells of the flowers toll' ('At Daybreak'). On the other hand, a swallow's nest is a faithful representation of paradise: 'On the inside / Immaculate and bright, / Lined with feathers //.../ On the outside, / A perfect camouflage / For what we call / With so much precaution / Death' ('Camouflage').

10, Serenela Ghiţeanu, *Cartea cu delfini. Convorbiri cu Ana Blandiana*, Bucharest: Humanitas, 2021, pp. 93-94.

The self feels the urge to retreat into safe, small spaces, 'Inside a Walnut', to penetrate the warm intimacy of the earth covered 'by layers of leaves / And the shadows of flocks / Of birds'. Yet for her, the concrete and immediate also exist on a spiritual plane. The sacred is contained in the earthly: 'This body / Is no more than the armour / That an archangel / Chose to wear to pass through the world' ('Armour').

The feeling of wonder pervades the landscape, leaves, plants, falling fruit, stars, and haystack – all take on a fantastic dimension, illuminated by mystery. Described in humorous riddles, the world would seem magnificent, were it not that, amid this jubilation of nature, the self is seized by metaphysical anxiety and the premonition of death. As before, the underlying motif remains sleep as both a substitute for death and a metaphor for the imagination. In the opening poem, we learn, 'Crickets only sing in their sleep / In daylight they're only bugs at play' ('In Sleep'). Similarly, poets only sing when they dream, and by day they live under the rule of 'dry and useless truth'. Tied to their own vocal 'strings', crickets make music of their lives. They sing at night, in their sleep, far from reality, filling the loneliness of the world with their song. Dreams, sleep or 'everything they'll never live' are the songs that will free them from 'the suspicious sincerities of day', helping them overcome existential emptiness. From the substance of dreams comes the poetry that gives meaning to life. For the world to regain its wonder, poets, like crickets, must forget their diurnal concerns in favour of the intimacy of night. In sleep, they cease to be common, and their ordinary selves 'die'.

Centred on nature and poetry, the poems in *The Cricket's Eye* advance definitions of mere being, of dreams and time, and of poetic creation. Landscapes have the simplicity of Japanese prints, vibrant with life and death. Blandiana dedicates a 'Hymn' to a tree: Its 'Fragile column holding up the sky, / The fruit of both evil and good', reveals the 'Inverted meaning of the worlds we can see.' In the orchard, 'Plums fall – one, two, three' and their 'kernels go down / Deeper and deeper into the ground / To reach, through greater pain, / A future life to come' ('One, two, Three'). These plums, fermented into alcohol, rotten and buried, become the protagonists of many poems, 'Their afterlife…the first spring', foretelling constant regeneration.

Indulging in philosophic daydreams, Blandiana nurtures wonder as the source of artistic creation. With the ingenuity of a child she asks, 'What if the sun and the moon / Are one and the same star / That the fear of the dark / Disguises [itself] as two different things?' ('Otherwise'). She cultivates a poetics devoted to the immanence of the miraculous. Like the Romantics, her mythic-religious thought draws from Platonic idealism. 'The wonder crackles beneath my feet, / Barely dressed in the / Form of wet branches', she writes, regarding all of nature – branches, rain, pine tree, the eye of the mole, fruit, roots – as the miracle that 'flows over stones' and 'drowses in the berries / And ripens them as they sleep'. Nature turns the tree into a candle that 'holds everything: Bees and butterflies, / Evil and good / In heaven and on earth'. ('Wonder'). The only thing alien to wonder is logic, that is, the obstinate self who pretends to dominate by explaining everything, to 'profane' it by analytical thought. In this way, Blandiana echoes Wordsworth in the *Lyrical Ballads* (1798) who exclaims, 'Sweet is the lore which Nature brings / Our meddling intellect / Mis-shapes the beauteous forms of things: – / We murder to dissect' and who concludes, 'One impulse from a vernal wood / May teach you more of man, / Of moral evil and of good, / Than all the sages can.' ('Tables Turned').

For Blandiana, any attempt to classify existence by means of logical thinking 'desecrates' the world's mystery. Knowledge comes by Platonic recognition, by remembering something that already exists: 'the important thing in poetry is not the new or the unheard-of, but something that we know from another life. Poetry should not aim to transmit knowledge, or cognition, but a feeling of re-cognition.'[11] Blandiana defines poetic knowledge as the discovery of what lies hidden in being. In 'The Egg' she reconstructs Plato's Aristophanic myth of the androgynous being from the beginning of time who was cut in two:

---

11. Ana Blandiana,'Between Silence and Sin', *My Native Land A4*, Hexham: Bloodaxe Books, 2014, tr. Paul Scott Derrick and Viorica Patea, p. 173.

Do you remember how we floated there?
Love with no yearning
Only reflecting itself, speechless
And content, like a spring,
Pain hadn't yet been invented,
Loneliness didn't exist.
The word was not yet born.

('The Egg')

Here Blandiana devises her own myth, an almost ekphrastic rendering of Brâncuşi's famous ovoid sculptures, 'The Newborn', 'The Sleeping Muse' and 'The Beginning of the World'. Evoking the unity of being before the creation of the world, when 'The word was not yet born', the egg represents a state of 'Love with no yearning', another figure for the game of life and death, the beginning and the end. Floating in a sea of light, the egg gives birth to heaven and earth, inaugurating a period of solitude that corresponds to the process of individuation. That process of being divided causes a 'wound' after the convulsive split of heaven from earth, which the tree's branches have tried to prevent by holding on to the sky:

The earth reached up into the trees
And the sky was tangled in branches
To cover the naked wound
Where they had broken in two.

The poet then wonders, 'Who has erred and how long will this error last?' before accepting the guilt. But separation gives rise to alienation, existential anxiety and uncertainty: 'The edge cut him in half, / reinventing us one by one.' The fragments in turn multiply to infinity, creating a world full of disconcerting illusions – heteroclite, promiscuous, threatening.

The drama of the divided self stirs a strong nostalgia for origins, leading to dim recollections of another existence and bringing Blandiana closer to the Platonic myth of the soul as expounded in *Phaedo*, *Meno* and *Phaedrus*. Wordsworth, in his famous 'Ode: Intimations of Immortality', refers to the pre-existence of the soul in an eternal realm, its birth on earth, the child's subsequent forgetfulness of its immortal origin as it grows, and the adult's faint memories of this initial state, memories that foster empathy with others. But Blandiana approaches this myth from a different angle, less interested in the descent of souls to earth or memories of pre-existence than in the journey that awaits the self at the end of life, for which she still feels unprepared:

> When I'm called, I'll have to know
> What to say, long before I go
> And what to do when I escape,
> For they cannot force
> Me to a new initiation,
> Make me start it all again
> With no preparation.
>
> ('One Day')

Blandiana rejects the abstract, the idea; she prefers the organic, since contact with the telluric has a regenerating effect. Plants, trees and nature are her guides. 'I'm tired of being born of the Idea, / I'm tired of not being able to die –', she confesses, trying to rediscover the biological roots of being ('I'm Tired'). Following the 'plant model',[12] she would rather be born from a leaf, in order to integrate herself into its seasonal cycle of death and regeneration. For her, the leaf represents 'the idea embodied in matter'.[13] Eternity and the abstract seem wearying and inhospitable. The 'plant model' offers a lyrical poetics of expiation and rebirth – with euthanasic overtones, inviting the poet to perceive death as an inseparable part of life, the agent of organic transformation. In this guise, extinction promises a happy, exultant experience, an endless fall that, having no end, transforms into 'flight'. The vegetal world with its eternal cycles, points the way to regeneration, where the boundary between life and death disappears, both coexisting in a primordial harmony which exorcises death itself. Again and again, Blandiana's speakers

---

12. Valeriu Cristea, 'Cu viziera zâmbetului', *Modestie şi orgoliu*, Bucharest: Editura Eminescu, 1984, pp. 58-61.

13. Dumitru Micu, 'Blandiana, poeta, după '89 (I)', *Nord Literar*, no. 2 (93), February 2011, p. 1.

14. Dumitru Micu, 'Lirism eutanasic', *Limbaje moderne în poezia românească azi*, Bucharest: Editura Minerva, 1986, pp. 253-269.

wish to link their destiny to the life-and-death cycle of fallen plums. For them, 'The rot is sweet, and fulfilment ends'… 'In the deep, dull thud of purple plums' where 'Life and death profoundly contend' ('Nighttime on a Bed of Hay'). The transition to death, in turn, restores primordial harmony and ensures the genetic cycle. Paradoxically, the fascinating world of life below earth offers enlightenment ('Illumination', 'There Are Some Mornings').

Many of the poems in *The Cricket's Eye* are preoccupied with poetry, poetic imagination, and the role of the poet, because for Blandiana, poetry as her inescapable destiny demands absolute devotion, a faith greater than faith in a god. She defines her own poetics as a hunt, although as she describes it, 'I've never hunted for words, / I've only searched for their long / Silver shadows, / Drawn across the grass by the sun, / Pushed across the sea by the moon.' ('The Hunt'). For Blandiana, the shadow embodies the aura, the trace of the miraculous in the concrete, and the suggestive power of the poetic word. As a hunter, she does not seek the word itself, but its ethical dimension, its metaphysical significance. Alluding to Adelbert von Chamisso's 'The Wonderful Story of Peter Schlemihl' (1813), whose protagonist loses his shadow as a result of his pact with the devil, Blandiana believes that 'its shadow is the most valuable / Part of a word / And that words that have no shadows any more / Have sold their souls' ('The Hunt'). Poetry, for her, is nothing if not mystical. Defining her poetics, she confesses that 'Poetry has given me a sense of the other in the world that surrounds us, that other that I would only call no one during moments of exhaustion.'[15]

The poet, on the other hand, is a mystic who recalls the words of St John of the Cross in *The Ascent of Mount Carmel* about the need to detach oneself from the things of this world: The poet, in her progress, renounces everything in a continuous loss of self:

> Memories, desires, passions,
> Love, and finally,
> When there's nothing left

---

15. Ana Blandiana, 'Between Silence and Sin', *My Native Land A4*, Hexham: Bloodaxe Books, 2014, tr. Paul Scott Derrick and Viorica Patea, p.172.

To cast away,
Not even a coat, however thin,
I take off my wrinkled skin
And the numbed flesh from the bone.
This is the great striptease
I carry out
Almost willingly.

('Falling')

Blandiana's poems never cultivate the play of forms gratuitously but penetrate the world's mystery longing for the absolute. Hers is a poetry that articulates the religion of love and immanence. Hers is an aesthetic seeking the very depths of existence: 'Poetry is not form,' she insists, 'but the sacrifice of form until all that remains is meaning.'[16]

VIORICA PATEA
University of Salamanca, 2024

---

16. Ana Blandiana. *Un arcángel manchado de hollín*, Barcelona: Galaxia Gutenberg, 2021, p. 460.

ACKNOWLEDGEMENTS

The translations included in this volume are of poems first published in book form in Romanian in Bucharest in these editions by Ana Blandiana:

Persoana întâia plural [First Person Plural] (Editura pentru Literatură, Bucharest,1964);

Călcâiul vulnerabil [Achilles' Heel] (Editura Tineretului, 1966);

A treia taină [The Third Sacrament] Editura pentru Literatură, Bucharest, 1969);

Cinczeci de poeme* [Fifty Poems] (Editions Eminescu, Bucharest, 1970)

Poezi* [Poems] (Editura Cartea Românească, Bucharest, 1974)

Somnul din somn [Sleep within Sleep] (Editura Cartea Românească, Bucharest, 1977);

Ochiul de greier [The Cricket's Eye] (Editura Albastros, Bucharest, 1981).

* The two asterisked titles arc selections, not individual collections, of poems that were added to anthologies and do not belong to a book of poems proper.

A full bibliography covering all her collections can be found on page 285 showing which volumes are included in which compilations of translations from Bloodaxe.

Acknowledgements are due to the editors of the following journals in which some of the translations from this book have previously appeared: *Chicago Review, The Cincinnati Review, International Literary Quarterly, New England Review, Notre Dame Review, The Riveter* and *The World Poetry Almanac*.

FIRST PERSON PLURAL

(1964)

Childhood

Out of the mirror, a skinny body stared
At me: ribs like a keyboard that clasped
My heart. It pressed against them gravely, as it dared
To see itself reflected in the glass.

My heart stayed hidden, but I knew it was there
Inside, like a game of hide-and-seek
(Just as the heart of the acacia nearby
Changes the essence of branch into leaf).

I wondered where it learned a song so deep.
I wondered if it always went the same.
In bed, at night, I was afraid to go to sleep
In case it stopped before the morning came.

Victors

First there was a storm in the fields out there.
We carried out our bows to vanquish its gloom
And came back triumphant, shaking the clear
Blue sky above the earth like a helmet's twisted plume.

I shouldered my cherrywood bow with pride
And marched in step with my joyful mates.
Dignified and silent, we dragged the dead
Cat of the mists, like a trophy, to the gates...

I came back, terrified, into the town
And joy balled up in our breasts like a cyst.
It was horrible, our spirits suddenly brought down
To see our desolate city like this.

The well-known ruins, stained by sunlight
Plucked out our eyes like burning tongs.
A landscape littered with huge jawbones,
Gaping holes – grotesque wounds we walked among.

The cherrywood bow on my shoulder rocked,
Ignored. We trod the rubble beneath our feet
With loathing, and heaved the dead cat of the mists in
Shock across a woeful slum of shattered streets.

Rain Chant

I love the rain, I love the rain with passion,
The madcap rain, the quiet rain,
The virginal rain and the rain like a hot-blooded woman,
The sudden shower and the endless, boring drizzle.
I love the rain, I love the rain with passion.
I like to wallow in its tall white grass,
I like to cut its blades and press them between my lips,
Let men get dizzy when they see me like this,
I know it sounds ugly to say that I'm 'the most beautiful woman of all'.
Ugly, and maybe not even true,
But let me, when it rains,
Pronounce those magical words: 'The most beautiful woman of all.'
The fairest because it's raining
And the locks of the rain look good on me.
The fairest because the wind is blowing
And my skirt is twitching nervously to cover my knees.
The fairest because you're
Far away and I'm waiting for you,
And you know that I am.
I'm the most beautiful woman in the world and I know how to wait
And nevertheless, I'm waiting for you.
The air is full of the scent of love in bloom
And all the passers-by are smelling the rain to take
In its perfume.
In rain like this you can suddenly fall in love,
Everyone on the street has fallen in love,
And I am waiting for you.
Only you know –
I love the rain,
I love the rain with passion,
The madcap rain, the quiet rain,
The virginal rain and the rain of a hot-blooded woman...

Harvest

The sky begins at the tip of the wheat,
As though each stem were crowned
With a brimful goblet of burning blue.
And the wind, as it pushes their foreheads,
Stirs the wine of the sky.

The sky begins at the tip of the wheat,
And when, beneath the scythe,
The stems bend over and softly fall,
It will be as though they bowed with reverence
To pour out their goblets of sky on the earth.

Pride

Who would dare to offend me?
My smile is burning hot at the core
Even when, frozen and still,
I make it a tool, and nothing more.

This happiness conjures birds
Even when my eyes go bleary.
Time snaps the hem of my dress
And I fashion earrings from cherries.

My lips like wings are beating
To lift my laughter up to the sky –
Laughter in waves, like liquid
Meadows of gold in billowing rye.

But joy is a serious stream
And in my childlike river-bed
Who would ever dare to offend
My generation's epaulettes?*

---

* Blandiana belongs to the so-called 'neo-modernist generation' or the generation of the sixties, the first that dared to break away from the enforced Soviet proletcult. They established a bridge with the tradition of the interwar period, previous to the Soviet parenthesis. [Tr.]

The Joke

The mischievous breeze has burgled the clothes of the trees
And scampers abroad, spreading them over fields and stones.
The newly-naked bodies of the trees in the rain
Are sobbing with undignified and tragic moans.

Withered and black, with disgusting skin, virility
Turned to wrinkles, and covered with ugly fuzz,
The shameless trees are a laughable burlesque
Of the salutary forest that one time was.

But under the knowing caresses of the rain
These vegetal satyrs begin to burn with sap
Like alcohol. Their hips commence to shake and roll
Around the rings of years. Dancing madly – springtime's hula-hoop.

Dance in the Rain

Let this rain embrace me from my head down to my toes.
Darlings, observe this new, new way that I prance
In the dark. The night hides passionate flowing
Winds, and the wind is the echo of my dance.

I climb the ropes of rain and find a place where
I can form a bridge between the stars and you.
I know that you love my serious, wind-blown hair
And you adore the flames of my temples too.

Gaze and gaze until your gazes come to the wind's new birth.
My arms, like naughty bolts of lightning in the rain –
My eyes have never glanced towards the earth.
My ankles have never been gripped by a chain.

May the rain embrace me and the wind destroy me!
Oh love this untamed dance I dance above your heads –
My knees have never kissed the ground in fee,
My hair has never known the stain of mud.

ACHILLES' HEEL

(1966)

The Gift

Tragic is my gift, like an ancient curse.
Which of my forebears sinned, for me to wear
His laurels and carry his guilt? Everything I touch
Turns to words, just as in the myth of Midas.

I feel close to that king who was killed by the curse
Of turning everything he touched into gold,
Only to starve to death because he couldn't eat
The golden bread and even had to gnaw on water.

I can't look up at the sky – it clouds with words;
How can I bite apples wrapped in colours?
Even love, when I touch it, turns into phrases.
Oh, woe is me, to be punished with praise.

Alas, alas, the trees don't lose their leaves,
Only old and yellow words fall in autumn,
The high mountains love them, but even the mountains
Quake beneath the weight of paired sounds.

I wish I could gather all the words in a single place.
I'd burn them to strip them from the world,
But the body of the world would shrivel up
Like the prince in the tale turned into a toad.

With them the world would also burn away
From the inside of the words, like an album…
Maybe I don't know how, or maybe it isn't possible to
Separate the world from the world of my present words?

Return

I come back home victorious from
The adventure of being honest.
How many generations since I left?
I don't recall and don't know where I've been.

I bring all the stars to show them
The garden they must warm,
And the mountains ask me to take them
To the place where they must raise their heights,

And the birds fly in circles and ask me
Where to build their nests, and endless herds
Follow my trail to find a place
To live in and multiply.

I say: 'Wait just a moment,
The place I came from is near,
A moment away, it has to be
Firm, a single firm place…'

But everything is flowing around me. I search
And I'm deathly tired of walking at the front,
Forced to hold firm inside of myself
The fulcrum of the universe.

I Know That Purity

I know that purity yields no fruit,
That virgins don't give birth,
And the great law of defilement
Is the tribute to life on earth.

Caterpillars grow from blue butterflies,
Fruit grows from the flowers all around,
The snow is an immaculate white
And the warm earth, impure ground.

The unstained ether sleeps,
The atmosphere is full of germs,
You can wish you were never born,
But you'll go into the earth if you were.

The word is content in the mind,
Spoken, the ear degrades what is named,
To which side of the scale will I
Incline, the speechless dream or fame?

Which will I choose, between silence and
Sin, the herd or the lotus flower?
Oh, the drama of dying in white
Or the death of winning for an hour...

At That Moment…

…At that moment the love of
Wild animals for their children begins.
Women should die when their young are born,
It would all be so beautiful in nature…
Tame and tranquil plants would grow
From their obedient hips that nestle pain,
Sweet snakes would crawl on the soil
Set down between their heavy breasts.
And fruits would blossom over the earth
Fed on mother's milk.
It would all be so beautiful.
From the trembling jet of sanctity
Women, smiling, would return to the elements…
But that's not how it is.
They aren't killed.
Just as Hamlet didn't kill the king
At his prayers,
Fearing
That he might, then, go to heaven.

Intolerance

Maybe I'm weak. And my eyes are weak.
I can't make out intermediate
Colours. I hate the sea;
It lets crabs fall in love with it.

I don't take a step beyond the blue frontier,
Fearing I won't know how to get back,
I curl up as though I were a worm in silk, where
I'm weaving purity around me like a cloak.

I want clear tones,
I want clear words,
I want to feel the muscles of words with my hand,
I want to understand what you are, what I am,
And clearly distinguish a laugh from a curse.

I want clear tones,
And colours in their purest state,
I want to understand, to feel, to see,
I prefer the clarity of my terrible disgrace
To this ambiguous felicity.

I want clear tones,
I want to say 'undoubtedly'
And not hold back, even when I have a break,
I hate transition, the pimply cheeks of
Adolescence only seem trivial to me.

Am I weak? Are my eyes weak?
Will I always be a ridiculous twit?
I hate the sea;
It lets crabs fall in love with it.

Parents

Parents always do everything for us –
They bring us into the world and help us to outgrow
Them, then they fade discreetly away
And leave us on our own.

Ashamed of being too old, too ill,
Too modest and too simple as parents,
They feel guilty for the wasted time
And watch us obediently in silence.

Later, they turn their gaze to a star in the sky
When its muddied beam grows thin shining down.
And tired, they wait no longer to
Lay foundations for us in the ground.

Quarantine

Pain is not contagious,
I can assure you it isn't transmitted,
Not a single twisted nerve in my neighbour's body
Tears away at mine.

Pain is not contagious, it separates
Us more effectively than walls,
No quarantine isolates us so completely.
It may sound banal – but this is the plot.

Oh Lord, how much literature we contain!
Sentiments – remember? – we learned them at school.
They all shed tears around the dying man's bed,
But no one is contaminated with death.

Stay calm, and selflessly care for the ill.*
Don't be afraid. You will not catch their pain.
He's dead. Does anyone want to follow?
Only the customary moans.

Oradea, 16/17 October 1964

---

* Soon after being released from prison, Blandiana's father died in hospital on 17 October 1964. [Tr.]

Hospital Visiting Hours*

Observe a moment of silence
For hospital visiting hours,
When all the hospitals in the world are waiting,
And the patients half-raise themselves in their beds
To see if the door will open for them.
That's when sweets and candies travel to hospitals,
Oranges roll there over the pavement,
Jars with jam and marmalade, chocolate –
So many metaphors for the love of friends.
The patients are forbidden to eat sweets
And they half-raise themselves in their beds
To see if their friends will come in.
But their friends are busy
And even if they came, the doorman guards the entrance.
All they can do – the patients – is wait, therefore
Observe a moment of silence
On Sunday afternoons from two to four.

---

* In Romania hospital patients could receive visits only from 2 to 4 pm. [Tr.]

Eclipse

I give up pity like a vice. They've drugged me
With pity since I was old enough to speak.
Doe-eyed, crown of stars, I weep silly tears
With the defeated, disinherited, the meek.

I weep for fools and fools defeat me.
Beneath my sterile star they smirk and grin.
My light is dying of tenderness;
Humanity and pity are doing me in.

I open tender hands, to caress
Wild beasts that hungrily creep near me.
It's sad to think I'll never kiss again
The snout that wants to tear me.

I've stifled myself, to avoid offending.
My knees have taken root in the ground
And my life has become a single wish:
Oh let these wings grow nails to grip me down.

The Change on the Table

I have an almost monstrous custom –
I hate owing anything to anyone.
I send flowers to the doctor who cures me,
Carnations for health
And we're even.
I leave the change on the table for the waiter,
If someone gives me a gift
I give them a bigger one in return.
When someone smiles at me – I smile back,
When someone makes a face – I also smile.
I close all my deals like this,
Always on top,
Burning all my bridges,
And sometimes
I get this crazy desire
To be grateful,
To crawl on my knees
And shout: 'I'm not worthy
To repay so much kindness, not even with my life.'
But in the end I always pay for everything.

Concert

I know I have to stay here in this seat
And make no noise, and not move around,
Quiet, as if I were nodding off to sleep
And didn't hear these swirling waves of sound.

I have a sinking feeling of defeat, as though
In a wood I'd seen a pair of wolf's blue eyes
And I can't defend myself. I'm stuck in the road.
And I love these wolves so I'm going to die.

I'm going to die because I love this melody
That strangles me while I hear.
I cut off my unshared emotion like an artery,
I hold it back like an eyelid holds back a tear.

It would all be changed if I could rip myself apart,
If the gates of my ribcage suddenly broke open here,
Enter me, music, come directly to my heart
Avoiding the damaged filter of my ears.

Or if I could cast off my body, like a pile
Of leaves in an old winter wind,
And keep only my pagan ears for a while,
With which, sounds, I would welcome you in.

I love you so much, I love you endlessly,
Please devour these broken bits of myself.
Oh art, this food will ennoble your mystery –
Your body of a youthful wolf.

Cruises

I know the planet's seas from cruises,
Almost-real departures into the world,
With giant waves and storms,
With strange birds and fish never seen before,
With plants of unknown colours,
With the watchful, fatherly eye of the lighthouse*
At our backs, enjoying our non-adventure
And the ship floating freely at the end
Of a hawser moored to the port.

---

* Allusion to the *Securitate*, the secret police who had the population under surveillance. [Tr.].

We Should Be

We should be born old,
Come wise into the world
Already able to choose our destiny,
Already knowing the pathways that lead from the crossroads of the
  origin.
Then, it would only be irresponsible to yearn to go ahead.
Afterwards, we'd gradually grow younger,
Come to the gateway of creation mature and strong,
Pass through, and enter into love as adolescents,
Then be children when our children are born.
They'd immediately be older than we are.
They'd teach us to talk; they'd rock us to sleep in a cradle,
And then we'd disappear, getting smaller and smaller,
Like a grape, like a pea, like a grain of wheat…

Torquato Tasso

He came to me from the darkness, the poet,
The poet undone by fear.*
He was beautiful. Like x-rays
Poetry passed through his form.
Poetry unwritten out of fear;
'I'm mad,' he said. In fact, I knew
It from the prefaces of his books,
But he carried his madness like a password
To enter into us, as though he had said,
'This is how I atone for
The absence of truth in my poems.
The cost is immense. Here I come. Receive me!'
But I responded, 'Get away from here!'

'I wrote in the light of the *autos-da-fé*,' he said,
'Feeling the rough shirt
Burning my flesh.
The windows in my room were the eyes of monks
And instead of doors, their ears, stuck to the wall
And the mice running from their holes were monks
And during the night huge birds in cassocks sang.
You have to understand...' And pointing a finger
He showed me the poems on my body,
Poems unwritten...
But then I shouted, 'Get away from here!'

---

   * Allusion to the Italian poet Torquato Tasso (1544-95) who rewrote his work to comply with the Inquisition. [Tr.]

Where Is the Pride?

What do I say? What's worth being said?
What's painful enough to shout about? And
Whose heart must I melt from lead
For something to grow in this sand?

What does the song that tames the
Beasts express? I could be Orpheus, true.
But what do I sing to the world?
In fact, I'm Eurydice too.

By singing I try to escape from death
But death is relentless, it has no end.
My belief isn't strong enough not to look
Back to see myself approaching from behind.

And so I get lost. Where is the pride
I have to have to believe that
Every word I pronounce
Will unleash planets in the sky.

And why this giving up of
The happy common slumber
If I cannot ring the deepest
Bell of the worlds, like thunder?

Is this too much? All of the mountains
On a strip of land, stacked high –
I want a clamour of human howls,
An answer to this cry.

To the Stars

All of the dogs in that country were loyal,
They only bit their masters' enemies,
They wore their leashes with style, like a necklace
(Their masters' wives debated what leash to buy them the following
    year),
So serious they only permitted themselves
A single whim: to howl at the moon.

(The moon, for dogs, is the country from which
Their forebears were once set free,
So a howl is a kind of
Epic song.)

But he was a very unusual dog.
He thought it was indecent to howl at the moon,
Because the moon was really his heart
Which he had to put back into his chest
Or die.

The other dogs warned him not to attempt it.
'It's useless,' they said, 'and anyway
They'll track you down and capture you.'
But he just smiled as he trotted off,
His paws voluptuously sinking into the sky,
Leaving a shiny, careless trail behind.
They never did catch him, because they couldn't
Follow his pawprints to the stars.

In the Great Silence

I feel sorry for those who are learning to be silent
And artistically mould their silence into shields:
Wisdom-silence, contempt-silence,
Humility-silence, mockery-silence.
They may seem better than me, bigger,
They never make mistakes like me, but nevertheless,
What fears their silences hide! Why
So many blocked-off bridges? Who are
They defending? I recall
How once, swimming underwater, I felt
A familiar sadness – in the great silence
I heard all the shells closing in my path.

Drawing in Pastel

Everything is old. Centuries old.
Snakeskins moulted long ago, in summer, crackle
Beneath my footsteps on the slabs.
What silence. I look around and only hear
The rustle of my wilting gaze in the air.
The dogs of the world have fled to newer ruins
And left the white pyramids in their nooks.
It is not rotten. Rot would mean vibration.
But time dries up in spite of the centuries.
Indifferent, the stone is sand
In stone –
Indifferent traces of footsteps, in this same place.
Dead columns, vault broken down and dead, watchtower
Dead, bridge and chapel dead, the wall,
The steps and the cellars. A beautiful
Blanket over everything.
Only the snow is alive,
Lustrous and white, the snow breeds worms!

The Surface of the Water

The feline leg beneath the dress
Innocently raised above the knee
And all the curves of being in that
One angle, gathered there sublimely

Do not inflame you, nor set off
Terrible short-circuits in your mind,
You no longer dream in the fiery night
Of the trembling steps of wolves tracking hinds.

From outside you can declaim each
Cell, you know it all at a glance,
Your lordly hand no longer moves
To caress me with bridal chants.

It's only the surface of the water.
We suddenly meet again, still alive and young.
The unknown within us is our food,
To satisfy us for centuries to come.

The Wisdom of the Earth*

She's large, patient and hard to budge, strike her
And she feels the pain in silence, with no tears.
She is large, which is why she doesn't move, she
Speaks only once or twice each hundred years.

We know she exists, that her body is big,
We know she supports us when we've transgressed,
We know she can't die, and we can always
Go back like children to her breast.

When the air is gentle and warm around us,
When we don't fear the wind, or fear each other,
We'll know it's the Wisdom of the earth that speaks,
The Wisdom of this earth, our mother.

---

* *The Wisdom of the Earth* (1907) is a sculpture in primitive modernist art by
Constantin Brancuși representing a naked woman seated with folded arms
around her legs that has come to symbolise Romanian identity. Brancuși
believed that 'Humility is the beginning of Wisdom'. [Tr.]

Be Wise

Do not fear my gestures,
You who can see me,
No matter how tempestuous my movements.
Be wise and rejoice.
Like an aeroplane's propeller I'm
Useless until you see me spin –
Only the peaceful place where the
Invisible propeller whirls is deadly.
Fear only the space where it seems
I don't exist and only weep in
The invisible wind that hides me.

Flow

Oh Lord, so much light flowing to the canal!
Let's lie down in the street to stop it with our
Bodies, its waves will break on us and
Erode us, like a shore.

We'll be naked from the start, since
The clothes we still have will rot away
From the splendour of the light and our
Unique bodies will be seen.
But little by little their outlines will shine
Like the light itself, indistinct,
And one by one beautiful pieces of body
Will leave us and scatter into the light.

Just as the shining sand in a violent storm
Abandons the beach and scatters into the
Depths of the sea.

Our forehead will be the last to go.
It will shine much longer than
The light in which it dies, leaving
Smoke above its hair, as a green flame
Flickers above some
Hidden treasure.

Oh, there will be more light then, much more –
The light that was before we came
Plus our bodies – all shall be well,
And thousands of bodies will wait for
Us, embracing purely on the cold asphalt,
To stop us from flowing towards the canal.

Self-portrait in Pastel

Disheartened by the satisfaction of the world,
My eyes are drier and my steps are a crawl,
And my every gesture ends where it unfurls,
And my baffled herds of horses die on the wall.

Oh, their whimpering neighs are much too childish
To be heard above the laughter in the distance,
My precarious sleigh no longer glitters as
It follows the downward course of existence.

Green herds born in vain on my walls,
In vain the snow storms fall on me there,
Disheartened by the world's satisfaction, I
Look for shelter with the terrible bears.

But my bears are as timorous as I am,
And smiling, I bleed in a lull of inaction
While, from the safety of the bears' thick fur,
Disheartened, I observe the world's satisfaction.

To the world's satisfaction, I am my bear and
The photographer standing beside my bear.
I do not bite, though I can bite. I do not bite
And I always take pictures of both of us here.

From Time to Time

I miss you from time to time
Like a bird misses the earth.
When I'm too tired of flying,
When my flesh seeks refuge in thought
And I feel that I'm rising to the sky
And I'm only the memory of a body,
I come back home to rest and
To be born a little again,
I founder, almost defeated,
And exhausted, I descend to the people
As great birds from time to time
Go back down to the earth to sleep.

Morning Elegy

At first I promised to be quiet, but then, in the morning
I saw you coming to the doors with ashes,
Sowing the ashes like wheat.
I could bear no more and shouted,
'What are you doing? What are you doing?'
I snowed on the city all night for you,
I made the dark night white for you: oh!
If you only knew how hard it is to snow!
I went out last night as soon as you fell asleep.
It was dark and cold. I had to
Fly off to the still point where the void
Makes the suns spin round and gutter out
And I had to make that angle flicker a moment more
To come back snowing for you.
I've thought out, weighed, tested, modelled
Every flake and polished it with my eyes,
And now I'm feverish and sleepy and tired.
I see you sowing the dust of the mortal fire
All over my white work and I tell you this secret with a smile –
Much more snow will come after me
And all the whiteness in the world will cover you,
From now on try to understand the law,
Gigantic snows will come after us,
And you won't have enough ashes,
And little children will learn to make it snow,
And whiteness will cover your weak denial,
And the earth will join the orbits of the stars
Like a burning sun of snow.

Volcanoes

There will be an age of the earth when
The flesh of stones will dry out and die.
In that autumn of the planet, as in
Any other, the forests will turn yellow.

But that yellow will be permanent
And slow, and will fade at last into grey,
And the sea will certainly waste away
And the sky will turn into cement.

There will be a hellish terror in things
Under ice from thousands of years ago
And the last of the plants will cling to
Life in the mouths of long-lost volcanoes.

Have I Grown Up?

Have I grown up? Are we mature?
How many thousands of shades rot a colour…
Dear and ridiculous, those days when I divided
The world into good and bad are gone.
We've come back strong from swimming in
This confusion, like Achilles in the River Styx,
But the fate of the whole world still
Depends on the vulnerable heel.
Everything is serious. And we understand it all.
From this moment on, time will pass unchanged.
We're adolescents yet, who haven't learned
The prudent fear of death.

From a Village

We all come from a village –
Some directly, others through their parents,
Some directly, bearers of myths and fairy tales,
The lucky ones able to go back when they wish.

Others, through their parents, get lost along
The slender, distant branches of the blood,
Rather than pastures, seeds and horses they know
The alcohol of the words extracted from them.

I want to retrace my parents' steps,
I want the village with the sound of my tear,*
The pathway through the fields of sleep
And the return of words into things.

I want to visit the cemetery with fallen crosses
And know that my footsteps are the same as theirs
And twine them into my ancestors' roots
Murmuring passionate words in my sleep.

But no one can tell me where I came from. Only
At night, when I wander the streets, do I feel close
To the metaphysical doormen waiting at the entrances
Of buildings, as though waiting on the benches of a village.

---

* A play of words impossible to translate. In Romanian 'lacrimă', 'tear',
alludes to the name of the poet Lucian Blaga's village, Lancrăm, and to the
title of his poem where he says 'My village that carries in its name the sound of
a tear'. [Tr.]

Scherzo

Soon I shall have a lovely sudden death, leaving
A deaf amazement behind, indifferent interim.
The wind, complicit, adorned in cheerful, breathing
Robes, will sing out a joyful requiem.

And winter, amused, will laugh as it snows
On my narrow Dacian* grave. Hearing it,
I'll imitate it in my mind, and slowly
Rock in the hammock of death, never fearing.

I'll play at beauty from time to time, and
Winding golden worms around my finger,
I'll spread black earth above my eyes in bands
Like the brim of a time-worn hat, and linger.

But when eternity carefully calls me
So I shouldn't by accident really die,
It will be too late. The boredom will enthrall me,
And I'll keep the dark hat on where I lie.

---

* The Dacians (Getae for the Greeks), the ancestors of Romanians, were a Thracian people inhabiting the territory of today's Romania and were conquered by the Romans in 101-102 AD. They believed in the immortality of the soul, and that death was just a passage to another mode of being. [Tr.]

I Gave You the Leaves

I gave you the leaves,
Please now give them back.
The earth around the trunk,
My gift too, give it back.
And the sap.
And the chance to bloom.
Everything I gave you before,
Now give it back.
Because you didn't understand
My butterflies,
Because they didn't make you glad enough,
My beautiful heralds of the end.

Night Is Falling

Night is falling slowly on my lips,
Night is falling slowly on my knees…
At least one star is born at every dawn
And horizons smile after begetting these.

Every mountain bears at least a mouse – *
The mountains of the world give birth submissively.
A general complacency assents to this,
While I just gnash my teeth.

May other horizons surround me,
Horizons that suffering makes much stronger,
And the mountains that cannot be eternal,
May they perish and live no longer.

May my modest eyes go down like the sun,
The peacocks surrounding me fade away,
Only let my barren cry be unbroken
On the edge of perfection, at the end of day…

---

* In classical literature from Aesop's *Fables* to Horace's *Ars Poetica*, the image of a mountain in labour which gives birth to a mouse alludes to grand promises, especially in literary and political contexts, which cannot be fulfilled. [Tr.]

The Day Will Come

The day will come
When I'll feel the need for leaves
And I'll heal myself with the grass,
When, getting older, I'll strap on bird-
Songs like an artificial limb,
When I'll need to take the moon
Like a pill on sleepless nights.
Don't worry. The day will come
When I won't be able to live without all of this,
When I'll be forced to acknowledge
The right of the universe
To be important.
The day will come.
But for now, by God,
Just leave me alone.

I Always Put Off Entering

I always put off entering words as though I were
Entering death, but I have no doubt I'll die,
Against my will, weeping for what I leave behind and
Wanting to turn back at each frontier on the horizon.

If only I had the risky faith of the Dacians,
Eager to find joy in death, then illumined,
With my forehead like a statue I would
Lose myself, smiling in the blessing of words.

If only I had the risky faith of the Dacians,
Believing every moment will give me back millennia,
If only I had the absurd faith of the Dacians,
So cruelly deceived after death…

Of Austerity and Naïveté

Like Racine, too young I left*
Austerity and naïveté,
Too young I cast the long grey cloak
Behind me, with a smile, into the past.

I was almost naked before the world
And, proud of my beautiful body,
I walk among stares like raised swords
And tear my halo to tatters.

I don't feel ashamed, though I'm often cold.
I still have no regrets, but I sometimes see
The stern black gate of the monastery in my
Dreams and the long warm, grey cloak

That forever wraps me in a cell
In my nonexistence while, barren
And sinless, I curse
The marvellous vanity of the world.

But – can't you feel it? – time unravels in me
And everything that was will be real:
Phèdre awaits me, and the king and the remorse
That, much too young, I left Port Royal.

---

*Jean Racine (1639-99) was educated at Port Royal, the Jansenist monastery famous for its strict, austere rules according to which the vanity of the world was anathema. He devoted his life to poetry and drama, but sometimes regretted betraying the ideals of purity for art. His best-known work is the drama *Phèdre* (1677). [Tr.]

THE THIRD SACRAMENT

(1969)

No Choice

Ushered into the great trial,
The one that ends by sending us to live on earth,
I was found to be innocent and
Given the right
To choose myself.
But I didn't want to be anything:
Not woman or man,
Or animal,
Not even a bird or a plant.
Out of the supreme right to choose
You could hear the seconds fall.
They plopped against the stone:
No, no, no, no.
Led to the great trial in vain.
In vain, I was found to be innocent.

Humility

I can't stop the day from lasting twenty-four hours.
I can only say:
Forgive me for the length of the day.
I can't stop silkworms from turning into butterflies.
I can only ask you to forgive me
For the silkworm, for the butterfly.
Forgive me if flowers turn into fruit
The fruit into seeds, the seeds into trees.
Forgive me if springs turn into rivers,
Rivers into seas, seas into oceans.
Forgive me if love turns into new-born babies,
New-born babies into loneliness, and loneliness into love...
No. I can't stop anything.
Everything follows its course.
Nothing consults with me —
Not the last grain of sand, not even my blood.
I can only ask you to
Forgive me.

You Know Something

All of you know something that
You don't want to tell me,
Yes, you know something,
Otherwise how could you have lived,
How could you have lived so many decades, you
My parents,
And you, the aged ones of the world?
Forgive me if I stop you in the street
Octogenarian.
Could you tell me too
That terrible mystery?
I kneel in the dense lava
At your feet, oh aged ones:
Please reveal the mystery…
The cold stars caress you with ill-fated claws
And you do not die.

Ties

Everything is me.
Show me a leaf that doesn't look like me,
Help me to find an animal
That doesn't moan with my voice.
Wherever I tread the ground it opens up
And I see how the dead, who have my face,
Embrace and give birth to more and more dead.
Why so many ties with the world,
So many compelled parents and descendants?
And why such maddening sameness?
The universe pursues me with my thousand faces
And my only defence is to lash out against myself.

The Bird

'I've been waiting for you,' said the bird, taking flight.
'Because of you I'll be late for the first time.
We could ask the sun to hold back for a while
But then we'd have to thank him.
Better to hurry up, hurry…
I'll tell you on the way why I called you
And who's waiting for you there.'
And she flew faster and faster,
And I had trouble keeping up,
I could see her speaking
But I couldn't make out what she said
And I couldn't remember
How we'd met.
Just once she turned her head
And then I understood:
'If I didn't tell you all of this
You'd be lost there…'
Then she moved her monstrous beak
And I had a feeling I shouldn't follow her,
Nor go on with this taxing flight that could
Lead to destruction.
But only by flying
Could I get close enough to hear
And then I was deafened
By the thundering sound of her wings.

The Borderline

I search for the beginning of evil
Just as, when a child, I searched for the edges of the rain.
I ran as hard as I could to find
A place to sit on
The ground and contemplate the
Rain on one side and no rain on the other.
But the rain always stopped
Before I could find its borders
And later it rained again before
I could discover how far the clear sky reached.
I've grown up in vain.
I still keep running with all
My might to find a place
To sit on the ground and contemplate
The line between good and evil.
But the evil always stops before
I can find the border
And it starts again
Before I find out how far the good extends.
I search for the beginning of evil
On this earth
That's sometimes cloudy,
Sometimes sunny.

Eye-blink

I don't dare to close my eyes for an instant.
I'm afraid
I'll crush the world between my lids
And hear it all crunch to bits
Like a hazelnut between my teeth.
How long will I be able to keep myself awake?
How long will I be able to keep the world alive?
I stare at everything desperately
And feel an unquenchable pity
For this helpless universe
That will end up dead in my eye when it shuts.

Oh, Laughing

Oh, laughing and crying and crying and sighing
We wake up celebrate gather take in
Till things are set and set until when
The great mime is free the sacred being

Till the very last step from the very first cry
All predestined in heaven on earth
But no one can know when we'll burst
Out suddenly laughing and crying and sighing our sigh

What double submission that very abyss
And the cats all listen and the dogs talk games
We save ourselves meet rise up and name
Just laughing and crying and crying like this

By Our Own Will

I began with little, not even guilt,
An incomplete gesture, a smile bitten off,
And what a disaster of beloved corpses we have now –
By our own will, by our own will, by our own will
Forbidden, punished, repressed.
Any sympathy with me from the trees
Disappeared long ago
And the sign from the spring that warned me
When it was poisoned.
What can I hope for when the birds fly away
Afraid to be near me
In case I kill them?
When snakes hide underground,
Worms in apples,
And the surrounding grass no longer dares
To shelter dead leaves?
When the universe, horrified, sees in me
A kind of submission it didn't engender?

North

We do not cheat because we're vile;
We cheat because we're incompetent.
We're lost in a fog and don't know
Who we are, and how.
Behind us, a line of unknown parents,
Before us, a line of unknown sons.
What do we know? Who do we know?
We move in jerks.
We take a step, then one step more,
And then another, and finally we're on our way
Looking back nostalgically at what we've left behind…
If at least we could get an answer to one question:
Which way is north?
On our foreheads our hair ruffles softly
As time
Passes by.

Travel

I walk around inside myself
Like I'd wander through a foreign city
Where I don't know a single soul.
At night I'm afraid in the streets
And on rainy afternoons
I feel cold and tired.
I have no wish to travel
Now that even crossing the street
Has turned into an adventure;
I have no memories of other lives
Before the question:
'Why was I brought to this place?…'

Only Love

Only the love between parents and children
Is seed.
You are my son, my love,
Everything stems from that.
Something indestructible
Flows between parents and children.
Don't cover your ears
With the laws of this world.
The entire universe is hanging
From this thread of blood that joins us
Like a holy sacrament.
Come close to me, like a child,
And kiss me, father, on the lips.

Requiem

Misunderstood, as only the things of childhood can be,
Definitely rejuvenated by departure,
For how many seconds of my life have I thought about
The man named Gheorghe,
The child called father?
He believed that mountains would suddenly
Grow legs like spiders*
And walk if they had faith:
Believed that in our chests under the soft bars of bone
We all have flocks of birds
Awaiting the happy moment when we
Decide to crush each other;
Believed that life, like buried seeds,
Would bring forth forests in future years...
Do not move your wings, angelical hosts,
Pronounce no truths beneath his eyelids.
Be good, little angels, let him sleep.
Be kind, big angels, let him believe.
Don't say a word, don't disturb him,
My naive father,
The tragic Gheorghe.

---

* Allusion to Mark 11: 23: 'For verily I say unto you, That whosoever shall say unto this mountain, Be thou removed, and be thou cast into the sea; and shall not doubt in his heart, but shall believe that those things which he saith shall come to pass; he shall have whatsoever he saith.' [Tr.]

Song

Leave me, Autumn, these verdant trees,
In exchange I'll give you my eyes.
Just yesterday, in the golden wind
The trees were weeping on their knees.

Leave me, Autumn, this placid sky,
The lightning on my face.
Just last night, the horizon tried
To scourge the trees in the grass.

O Autumn, leave the birds in the air
And banish instead my footsteps' marks.
This morning the vault of heaven
Bled with the cries of larks.

Leave me, Autumn, the grass, and
Fruits and leaves, and bears
Still unasleep, and storks still here,
The shining hour.

O Autumn, leave me this day,
Shed no more smoke towards the sun.
And let your evening fall on me,
My sun is setting anyway.

Love

Love, fear of loneliness,
Ambiguous deity
Buried to your waist in the earth,
I ask nothing of you.
All of the leaves fall for me
And the birds come close to me
When they leave.
The stones mate before my eyes
And give birth;
What more could I ask you for
Implacable Mistress?
Above the pristine snow
For me at least
The seraphic bones of the birches
Will remain…

The Docile Animal

What a docile animal the universe is!
Planets circulating
Like red and white blood cells,
Suns burn them – temporary cauldrons
On the brain…
We are its eyes,
Which he opened late
Like the eyes of a cat,
The fragile eyes he protects
With care and infinite despair.
We are the eyes,
The eyes that can do nothing
But see.

Ancient Anchorites

Ancient anchorites in the woods,
Wolves' hides stuck to their skin,
Eyes and ears woven
Shut with hair
And beehives growing in their tangled beards.
They do not remember why they came
And they long ago forgot the word
They were supposed to shout to the world.
At times, a sign of heaven's will
Descends in the body of an eagle,
But the old men only play,
Braiding flowers into the feathers of the bird,
And an angry God cannot understand
That they have forgotten to hate.

I Hope

…It will be a gentle and childish morning
And the light, as it passes, will
Crackle in the leaves;
And the room will smell
Of newly-sharpened pencils
And paper yet unused;
And I'll wake up from thoughts,
Or love or only from sleep
Happy, in a daze,
And will sling a jacket over my shoulders
And go outside feeling silly,
Feet without stockings in my shoes
And happily ask:
'Does anybody know what year this is?'

Grass

I yearn for tall grass,
The grass on the edges of cities
Where the knee of the earth
Swollen and shameless
Is covered with dead dogs
And empty tin cans.
There the grass grows tall and free
Soft, useless, unaware.
Then it slowly withers and doesn't understand
That it won't exist any more.
And everything happens simply and painlessly
And not even in the worst of nightmares
Is the word
Eternity
Whispered in an ear.

Far Away

The creature that bears my name
Moves around among us,
I always see her
From far away –
A tenuous silhouette
Or a surprising gesture.
I hear her laughing
And I hear my words
Spoken from her mouth
Like strangers.
I, defenceless,
A thousand miles
Away

Condition

I am
like the
sand in an hourglass
that can
only
be time
when
it falls

The Eyes of Statues

Do not make me a caryatid in a temple!
Look at me closely and be horrified.
How foreign my body is,
Denying the marble.
My fingers tremble
And my mouth is dry with fear,
I always feel I'm being called
And I shudder,
I don't know what to do with my hands,
I have fever,
And with every breath
I wince with pain.
Only my eyes – yes, I admit it, my eyes –
Are like marble,
White,
But with the pupils looking inward.

Psalm

Behold, my cautious father,
The cranes betray, the trees surrender,
Wisdom spreads.
Will you be satisfied?
This is what, word for word,
They taught me not to say.
But, Lord, will you promise
To keep my words alive
In this silence,
So that the birds will know how to come back,
And the leaves will find
The branches they fell from,
So that everything will be able to rise again
Then, when you are strong enough
For me to ask:
Will you turn my sadness into hate?

Fatigue

What docile dead we have!
They don't erupt through volcanoes,
They do not budge beneath the walls
Constructed above them,
They let themselves be locked up in statues
With gestures sculpted by others,
They let themselves be harnessed in banners
On unfamiliar roads,
They let themselves be shown and they rot
Conscientiously to nourish the earth.
What docile dead we have,
And so very tired.

While We Still Have Time

Take fresh words and pronounce them
Until uniform and polished
And no one remembers
What form and meaning they had before.
When all the living words have been extinguished
Someone will be lurking to avoid new ones being born
And if, in spite of everything, a new word appears
They'll repeat it and repeat it until
No one can remember it.
Then
They'll call in scholars
Specialised in discovering lost meanings
And they'll take an old man to a lab
And ask him if he remembers
The meaning of some word.
And he'll mumble, hoarse and uncertain,
'Who knows, maybe my grandfather…'

While we still have time, let's hide the living words,
Save the words that still have breath,
You, who are forced to listen,
You who for centuries have been
The docile witnesses to the crime…

Alternative

What a long, long time
God needs
To admit
That Satan exists!
With a simple nod of the head
He would've won the battle.
He only has to say
That he created it,
Confess to
The decisive see-saw
On which
Because of Satan's weight
God always ends up
On the side of the board
Lifted into the air.

Elegy*

Bandage my naive wounds
Lady, lovely and kind,
The wounds through which my faith has flowed
Moment by moment, a month, from my mind.

Place light leaves that no longer hate
And will never love again
Like gauze on my forehead
Yellow Lady forgiven.†

Bind my ears with rustling wings
To forget the roaring engines
Of the planes, and gently cover my eyes
To keep me from trying to comprehend.

Let rain bathe this body, though which
Like a plough, amazement passed,
And let the deep red tongues of the grass
Lift me onto the pyre at last.

Have mercy then, and call on the snow
To crazily fall, and fall some more,
And the claws of birds to lay down
Pious crosses in the snow.

---

* This poem, written following the Prague Spring, is a lament for the Soviet invasion and an invocation of history, the Lady named in the text. Blandiana viewed the rebellion of the month of August with enthusiasm, but describes it in autumn, when everything had ended in tragedy. The season itself is a metaphor for the loss of hope.

† 'A woman forgiven', in Romanian, refers to a woman who has experienced menopause. [Tr.]

Everything simple

If only I were a candle
I could slowly burn away
From one end to the other
Simple, as in schoolboys'
Arithmetic...
First my head – what joy! –
Would disappear,
And everyone would say
'This girl has no head!'
I'd just forget about it all
And try not to understand anything else.
My heart would melt,
I'd love no more,
I'd hate no more,
And suffering couldn't reach me,
And everyone would say:
'This girl has no heart!'
And from that moment
On, I'd have no desires,
No passions,
And the ships of my blood
Would scatter away
And I'd only have my dried-up knees,
Trembling with dignity or bent to the ground.
No one would bother to say a thing.
In the ultimate silence,
The puddle of wax
Would cool down, punished
By all the terrible shadows that
Its light has brought into the world...

Indecision

Everyone lives two or three, or even four lives at once.
We are born so young,
Oh Lord,
That out of a thousand potential lives,
It's impossible to pretend
That we're able to choose just one.
The animals of one life prey on the animals of another.
The fishes of a larger life feed on the fishes of a smaller one.
Self-destructive, the branches of the trees dry out at their tips.
The sun of the fourth life darkens
The sun of the third; the sun of the second
Darkens the sun of the first.
Conflicted with themselves, our lives cancel each other out
And, still undecided and immature, we die.

Contretemps

I look at the past and I don't understand
The footprints I've left behind.
I look at the frozen snow
Which (I remember) injured
My naked feet.
But those prints form signs
In the alphabet of a vanished language.
Yesterday what I wanted to say
And tomorrow, how will I read
The pain of walking now,
When the thickened seconds
Seem like years and the years, epochs,
Inconclusive and endless
No answer is born
Except when no one needs it
Any more
And the question that awaited it
Has died.

The Fall

The prophets died out in the desert
And angels, dragging their wings on the ground,
Were placed in rows in the squares.
Soon they'll be tried
And asked: What sin
Got you thrown out of heaven?
What guilt? What betrayal? What mistake?
They, with their last drop of love,
Will look at us, bleary-eyed with sleep,
And they won't find the devilish audacity
To confess that angels don't fall
Because of sin – not because of sin,
But because they're just worn out.

Pietá

Lucid pain, death has brought me back
To your arms, submissive, almost a child.
You don't know whether to be grateful
Or to cry
For this happiness,
Mother.
My body, torn from the husk of the mystery,
Is yours alone.
Your sweet tears drop onto my shoulder
And gently press against my neck.
How good it feels!
The misunderstood wanderings and words,
The disciples you are proud and afraid of,
The father, intuited, not spoken of, is watching,
Everything is over now.
Calmed by the suffering you understood
You cradle me in your arms
And, in silence,
You gently rock me.
Hold me, Mother.
I only have three days to rest
In death and in your lap.
Then resurrection will come
And once again you won't understand.
Three days only
But until then
I feel so good
In your lap, brought down from the cross,
And, if I didn't fear to frighten you,
I would turn my mouth
To your breast, and suckle.

FIFTY POEMS

(1970)

Encounter

Don't be afraid.
It will all be so easy that
You won't even understand
Until much later.
At first you'll wait
And only when you
Start to think that
I do not love you any more,
It will be hard for you.
But then I'll plant
A spear of grass
In the known corner of the garden
To grow
To where you are
And whisper:
Don't be afraid
She's well
And waiting for you
Just there – on the other side of me.

Let the Words Fall

Let the words fall
Only like fruit, only like leaves
Only those that are ripe with death.
Let's let them fall
Almost rotten,
The sacred bone
Barely dressed in their flesh.
The naked core opened,
Maybe it would slip, as the moon
Slips from the clouds, towards the ground.

October

They drip onto my forehead,
Warm tears
And cool,
Softly
Onto my eyelids,
As though they sprang from
My own closed eyes.
Who is crying above me
And turning
His sweet tears
Into mine,
Father
Or maybe a stranger
Who adopts me this way?

Frost

Very soon I will forget how to speak
Till then
Even the seconds will have
Names so long that
They can't be pronounced in a second…
The frost on the broad leaves listens
What peace there will soon be,
When no one will be able to tell
Who's listening,
Or who could pronounce a word.
Frost on ample leaves.

Up There

Up there on the mountain a house
Appears and disappears among the clouds.
Who wraps it in such cowardly shields
And then so often removes its shrouds?

Who makes it prey to our eyes
And who makes our eyes its prey?
We hang from that humid icon like
Tears in the lashes of gods unnamed.

Do we remember it from another life
Or is it only a horrible foreboding?
But we live, if we live, to see it up there
On the mountain, seemingly floating…

Psalm (II)

You who taught the bears to sleep
The winter through,
Why won't you teach me what sleep is?
I'm not asking you for everything
You know that
I'm too modest for death.
But who, sailing
Above my open eyes,
Wouldn't beg you for
A wind of nothingness?

---

   * **Death in the Light** *(see opposite page)*: A reference to Emily Dickinson's poetry 'Will there really be a morning?' (J101/Fr147) which Blandiana translated into Romanian. (Tr. Note)

Death in the Light

1

You know
How much silt and mud
The flowing waters of the day leave
In me and what heroic darkness I need
To wash them away
And how,
When my eyes have barely forgotten
The foreign forms of the bodies
And not a single ray of light
Disturbs the profound vision any longer,
My frightened ears
Begin to distinguish
The flowing of time
Back to the light of day once more.
Impelled,
The darkness takes shape,
Becomes impure and moves.
Rising up from the snow,
The dog hears something,
The guard begins to button
His coat.
Help, I cry,
Hoping that someone
Can stop him.
And what if
The morning doesn't return?*
I ask, hoping
That someone can still help me.

---

* A reference to Emily Dickinson's poetry 'Will there really be a morning?' (J101/Fr147) which Blandiana translated into Romanian. (Tr. Note)

What if everything stopped moving?
What if the huge wheel
That drags me through the day
Stood still?

    2

Father, it only depends on you,
It only depends on you that,
In the warm cradle
Where you alone gave me birth,
You come to me.
You made my arms
And I find you in the dark,
And my breath
You only feel it in the night
Close to your thin collarbone,
And your eyes only see me through the darkness,
And I feel so good,
And you feel so good.
My beloved Lord, my father and my brother,
Do not cast down the light on me so that
I disappear into its devastating whiteness.
Don't be afraid of me!

    3

If the morning didn't come,
If the slippery cusp of the night
Didn't always vanish beneath my feet,
Who would dare to demean
My nightly ventures,
The endless loneliness in which
I can sometimes feel you coming near
Only to struggle and break away.
Is it a sin, Lord, to hold you like a trap
Inside of me to be able to caress you?

4

Who would dare to come to my aid
Against your will?
The sun only listens to you
And with the sun
Forests of eyes
Grow up around me,
Comforting, humble and wet.
Help me, help me,
Only you can command them to sleep,
Only you,
My brother whom I never encounter,
You,
The groom of my quest,
You,
Who covers your ears with your wings
So that you cannot hear me.

5

I have never been more mortal
Oh, your thorns sink sweetly into my shoulder,
You're too close
To feel the pain
When you softly lay your head on my chest,
Night is falling above the calendars,
I rock you, father,
In my cradle
And I want to smile
When I remember
That my obedient son is God.
But the night makes him grow and makes him my brother
And he soon forgets he's my brother,
Close to his slender collarbone
My sacred mouth breathes
For an indecisive moment.

And then
You become my father again.
What ancient terror
Before I came into the world
Makes you call the dawn upon us?
You were happy
When you gave me birth.
What nostalgia for the power you had
Before you loved
Makes you
Twist the light in both of us?

6

The forests around me have eyes,
The place of the dog is drawn in the snow,
The guard sleeps somewhere in the sun.
More and more deadly,
'What a pity!' I murmur, and I do not understand
Whether I mourn for the sin
Or only hoped it would come.
Pure, I await the next night
And the next death in the light.

The Soul

The soul is something inside of us.
It can't exist on its own.
How often has it happened:
I discover naked souls, dying in the grass...
I carefully gathered them in my hands,
But I couldn't find anyone quickly enough
To take them as they were,
I felt that my palms were empty
And a mist, untouched by the leaves, passed
Suspiciously through my body.
Does the soul take refuge in us
From God?

FROM

POEMS

(1974)

Genealogy

Someone is dreaming us
Dreamt in turn
By someone else –
The dream
Of a certain
Dream.
Absorbed in somnolence
We also dream of a savagely
Tormented world in our sleep.
Dreaming
We form one tender link
Of a chain with no beginning that
Will never
End,
Though
A single cry
Would suffice,
If loud enough, to half
Awaken
The primal Lord
Of all sleep,
Asleep at
The foundations of the world
In a dream.

Every Movement I Make

Every movement I make
Is reflected
In several mirrors at once,
Every look I take
Meets itself
Repeatedly,
Until I forget
Which one is real
And which an imitation.
Mistress,
I'm afraid to go to sleep
And ashamed
To be.
For me
Every sunrise
Has an unknown number of suns
And one
Soothing
Day.

I'm Drowsy

I'm drowsy, like
The fruit in autumn,
I'm drowsy and I feel fine,
I'm good, I'm warm,
The bees are buzzing
In my mind,
My head will nod on my shoulder
Soon,
Just like any fruit
That suddenly falls
And begins to rot
On the ground.
I slip into sleep
And my head begins to rot
With dreams,
Softly yielding
Spirits sweet,
While, in its turn, an angel-worm falls asleep
And begins to dream
As it rots away.

The Ballad of the Custom-house*

Don't be afraid, you told me,
The god of the colour of withered leaves
Will show himself at the custom-house of sunset.
He has
A songbird's beak,
Moans are enclosed in his ear
And his eye is open like the dead.
Fawns and
Deer go with him,
They advance in pairs
Like kings
With crowns made of rings of wilted grass –
He'll take you to the custom-house of the northern frontier.

An aged god
Awaits you there –
The clouds exude
From his right eye,
From his left eye
Twilight is born,
His back is bent and his head is bald,
His mouth has a twisted grin and
He hatches serpents' eggs beneath his arms,
Crow-feathers grow from his shoulders,
And fishy fins from his elbows,
His hoarse voice croaks at times –

---

* In Romanian popular belief, when someone dies they must go through
different 'custom-houses' where they are judged and have to pay for the sins or
errors committed in life. On the third day the soul sets out on the road to
heaven, but it has to pass through several custom stations of the air where the
evil spirits reveal the sins it committed by word. For example: at the second
station, lying; at the third, slander, and so on. [Tr.]

That voice will go with you
To the custom-house of the rising sun.

From there
A child who is hiding
Will guide you.
That child is a god, but refuses to admit it,
He sometimes turns into a lark
Or a frog
With dandelion whiskers,
Butterfly wings,
Twigs for horns
And the humped shell of a snail.
You can only
Tell it's him
By the bitter line
Of cranes
That follow
Behind the faint ray of light
Wound thrice
Around his body,
After the hurried trembling
Of the mulberry leaves.
Make haste.
Let him pursue you, you whispered,
To the custom-house of the southern frontier.

But do not wake up, you shouted,
The mistress of the entire kingdom
Awaits you there.
She will pass her hand over your eyes,
Have no fear,
Keep in mind –
She is the fairy
With the shrill voice of the peacock,
With the smell of strawberries,

With skirts of mandrake leaves,
With green lips
And hair of delirious water
Flowing towards the sea;
Birds fly through her body,
Fish swim through her hair –
Do not wake her up!
Lizards shed their skins,
The sun is blind in her hand
And doesn't light the day,
Only the bitter moon
Drips from on high
Above us...
If you have the strength
To dream that you're asleep, you said,
You can return
By way of the custom-house of the setting sun.

My Beauty Hurts Me

My beauty hurts me,
Less familiar than the moon
Moving from mirror to mirror,
From pool to pool,
Always an icon
Unshakeable,
Though it doesn't completely
Fit into sleep.
It moves from world to world
As if
It were myself,
But more like smoke,
Certain
To remain an icon
Forever,
Inexistent, like the moon on pools of water.

Ballad

Lady Nature,
Lord God,
Even
Those who
Have known him
Hold their tongues.
His hands feed words
To the birds,
Keeping nothing
For himself,
Not a prayer,
Not a slur.
He remains alone
As spotless
As an unborn child.
Letter-seeds,
Syllable-branches,
Word-seasons
Fit into his eye,
But
In vain –
Only the bees
Know how to drink
From his tear,
Only the butterflies
Can bury us.

Syllables

At times I try to press out
My voice, like a deer that hides,
Somewhere deep inside,
A unicorn's inscrutable crest.

Amazed, I hear how my clumsy pondering
Changes into deities and kings
Who talk among themselves, chatting
In a long-forgotten tongue.

Unfamiliar syllables gather round my heart
Without my intervening,
Relentless, superb and preening.
No longer surprised,
I listen, I wait, alert,

And I count how, cold and sparse,
Death and my eternal existence
Drip from my rounded lips, in the distance,
As though they came from the stars.

Between Worlds

I move from one life to another
Softly stroking
The mane of the sleeping lion
At the entrance.
He's used to me now,
To my eternal disappearances at dawn,
To my eternal returns
At twilight.
Defeated, at times,
I cannot manage to reach him.
Then he gets up,
Tenderly
Takes my head between his jaws
And slowly drags me.
At other times
I don't know how to get back from my dream.
Then he follows me
Into the maze
And tells me
With roars
That he'll save me,
That I must wait motionless
In my memory
So he can find me
And take me
To his kingdom.
Oh, his marvellous kingdom,
Fragile land,
Delicate frontier
Of hours
Between two worlds that devour each other
In a ceaseless
Tug-of-war.

Maybe Someone Is Dreaming Me

Maybe someone is dreaming me –
And that's why my gestures
Are so soft
And blurry,
As though they forgot their purpose
In the midst of every motion,
Grotesque,
That's why my figure is fading,
Second by second,
And my actions dissolving...
And maybe whoever is dreaming me
Is shaken from time to time
Out of sleep,
And wide awake,
Taken back against his will to real
Life,
And that's why I'm going dim,
Hanging at times
As though from a dissolving thread of snow,
Not knowing
If I'll ever go back to sleep
So that something else
Can happen to me.

When I Wake Up

When I wake up, snow
Will be covering the books and
The carpet with beauty
Around my head,
Like a diadem on the pillow,
A weightless sheet on my skin.
Enormous snowflakes will fall
In the quiet room
Like the souls of dandelions,
Dropping so slowly
From ceiling to floor
It will take them an eternity.
Then I'll see ancient birds
With their deformed feathers raised –
How long will I have slept
For so much snow to fall?
Or maybe, in the meantime,
I'll have died.
And I'll get up to
Run away in fear,
But the birds will screech
In a kind of guffaw,
Pointing with their wings
To where my feet
Have left no footprints in the snow.

Prayer

To lie face up in the snow
With open hands,
Like a cross of untold beauty
Purposely
Immersed in sleep,
Upon which only angels would deserve
To be crucified
For the sins they committed
In heaven.
White with no edges
And peace with no beginning,
Clouds dispersing into flowers
Cover me softly with snow
While burning tears
Are born under eyelids closed
And freeze before they can flow
From these dreams.
Amen.

SLEEP WITHIN SLEEP

(1977)

Hills

Sweet, forested hills – spheres
Whose other half is hidden in the earth
So the dead can also enjoy
Your round voluptuous flesh.

Right now maybe one of the dead is listening,
Like me, as eternity passes by,
Remembering lost lives, one by one,
And whispering as he stares at you:

Sweet, forested hills – spheres
Whose other half is hidden in the sky
So the living can also enjoy
The endless sweetness of your breath…

Poem

Who and what can we dream of
In this time grown over us –
Heavy snowdrifts of sleep
That lunatic heroes
Try to shove away
With valiant gestures?
Don't shout,
Waking would kill them.
You only need to weep
To see them –
Timid
Proofs
Of the death yet to come.

Eyelids

Always trembling in the all-embracing silence,
Struggling, exhausted
Poplar leaves,
Millions of weary
Eyelids,
Hiding
The solitary eye,
Myopic and tearful,
That we feel burning into
Our backs
When the eyelids of the poplar
Are blown away by the wind.

In Winter the Stars

In winter the stars
Are so far away
They can't be seen
In their lonely array.

In winter the seas
Are such foreign things
They don't have a right to
The waters of the springs.

In winter the dead
Are so cold and sear
That it freezes forever
The earth's hemisphere.

Shepherd of Snow

I'd like to be a shepherd of flakes of snow,
To have the care of swirling herds for a time
And shepherd them through the infinite sky
And bring them back home, whiter than before.

To watch, on tinkling nights, and be one
With the lonely sobbing of the moon,
Cast back from the temple wall of the clouds,
As my life goes by and the white flocks drowse.

I'll wait until the heat of summer slays
My lambs to give sweet earth its needed libation
And then, as decreed, we'll all flow away
In immaculate, intended transmigration.

Native Land

I've never missed anyone else in you,
A land that sinks like sunsets into dreams
Through circling orbits of green,
And I become an exile if I cross the frontiers
Of your weary hair.
I can only speak your language
In my sleep
And only spin out stories just for you,
My ever passing paradise,
My ever passing owner,
Always you.

Outside, it's growing cold.
The fog is getting thick, and
Night is coming on.
Time goes slowly by,
But it's so cosy here at home
Where each of us keeps the other's native land.

A Stork's Nest

Lonely stork's nest on a chimney top,
Gatepost holding up a broken flowerpot,
Meaningless pictures return to the walls
Of my mind and burn.

I've never really seen them. Maybe I acquired
Them at my mother's breast. I don't know why
I recall them – an obsession that arrived
In the nourishing milk I imbibed.

But whenever it snows they appear
As if they were always waiting there,
Broken stork's nest, flowerpot forgotten below,
A deserted village about to be buried beneath the snow.

As Though the Moon Had Something to Say

As though the moon had something to say
About this love and hate that bind me to the snow
She began to write bright letters
On her snowy mantle
That she herself erased.
It could have been a threat
Or maybe some advice,
But something important was being transmitted,
The words shone and screamed
On that empty field
Like peacocks –
I had to answer,
Darkness held its breath,
The pale snow waited,
Everyone believed that
I understood
The dead language of the moon…

Hostile Snow

This snow is hostile,
It's falling with hatred
On waters frozen by hate,
On fields that flower with evil,
On bitter, resisting birds.
It's snowing as though
It had to wipe out
The life of these aquatic people.
It's snowing with a human
Inclemency,
Sharp, stinging flakes.
Who could be surprised?
Only I know
That the snow
Of the beginning was love.
It's so late now
And this snow is hideous,
And all I can do
Is wait
For the hungry wolves,
To be their fodder.

Wings

Churches don't have roofs
But wings made of tiles folded close to
Their bodies.
The day will come
For them to extend their wings
And rise up
Slowly, against their will,
Lifting their bodies
Of gold and smoke
In the sky above,
Roaring through the air, like
A flock of heavy birds
Towards the West,
While hysterical mountains
Mixed with the sea
Gush up and collide
And tumble down –
Beautiful end of the world
Beneath a blue, vivid sky
Teeming with living churches.

Avram Iancu*

Playing his voiceless flute, the defeated prince
Of our dreams advances all alone,
Behind him grow vast forests of lament
For endless disasters, echoing with moans.

Behind him lies our sleep-shattered land,
Ploughed only by earthquakes, on its own
Beneath the blood-red shudders of day, and
Sown with ancient, princely bones.

If only his flute could cry out loud, the sound
Would call warriors from the disgusted ground,
But his helmet is a swarm of somnolent bees
And his armies are lambs, sleeping at their ease;

But grapes get drunk and sleepy on their vines;
Clouds doze in the sky and waves on the lake,
Grains drowse off and fall before their time,
All beneath the poppy's heavy weight;

But rivers nap in their beds, and leaves sway
Asleep in the trees, an entire country tranquillised
In dreams, while the sleeping prince walks on and plays
His voiceless flute with empty, open eyes.

---

* The son of Romanian serfs, Avram Iancu (1824-72) was a lawyer and revolutionary who led the uprising of the Transylvanian serfs, the Moti, in 1849 to free them from serfdom. Transylvania belonged at that time to the Austro-Hungarian Empire but was governed by Hungarian noblemen. Avram Iancu could not ally himself with the Hungarian revolutionaries of 1848 because their leader, Lajos Kossuth (1802-94), denied rights to other ethnic groups such as the Romanians, who represented the majority population in Transylvania.

I Hear

I hear someone walking behind me on the moon,
Putting down flower seeds along my trail,
One right step – a pretty bluebell,
One wrong step – a banewort, or broom.

I hear someone walking behind me on the sun,
Putting down birds' eggs along my trail,
One right step – a dove, or a quail,
One wrong step – an oriole, the singing one.

I hear someone behind me in eternity,
Putting down words in my tracks,
One right step – quotation marks,
One wrong step – poetry.

Therefore, Iancu had to fight alongside the Austrian and Russian troops. He refused to receive the praise of the emperor, who wished to decorate him in recognition of his help in bringing victory to Austria. Instead, Iancu withdrew to his people and ended his life alone and depressed. He wandered through the forests like a mountain spirit, playing the flute, and lived on the alms he received. Bees and lambs are characteristic symbols of Romanians and their ancestors, the Dacians, whose direct descendants were the Moti of the Apuseni Mountains. Together with Horea, who led the 1784 revolt in Transylvania, Avram Iancu is the symbol of the liberation of the Romanians. [Tr.]

Hymn

I left a stalk of hay in the shade, glowing
Brighter than the light of the yellow leaves
On the walnut tree between the sun and me.
They were naked and frail from so much breathing air.
I lay on the drying grass and looked up at the sky,
No thoughts, no wishes, no words,
Just smell, and hearing, and sight,
And waited for twilight to come.
For hours I was body, nothing more,
Lost in deep aromas, like a happy
Fruit that the flow of time has ripened and
Made sweet, ready for decay.
The only sound was the rasping rustle
Of the almost wooden walnut leaves, falling endlessly,
While in the sky, surprised and timid stars
Took the place of moving constellations of birds.

Everyone Living in the Village

Everyone living in the village was asleep.
The knowing aroma of quince, like a mist
Had drugged them so deeply, they
Might have dreamt that they didn't exist.

Soft and heavy stars dragged down
The ripened sky to the ground
As if the day of the hereafter impended,
As if it were ready to be fermented.

Stars too sweet from so much love,
Fruits that were rotten with desire
Out of which the end of the entire
World softly trickles into jugs.

Sweet rains of murdered plums in heaps,
The knowing aroma of quince like a mist,
Everyone living in the village was asleep
And might have dreamt that they didn't exist.

Song

I write this song with a berry on leaves,
Behind me, hordes of ants will drink it here;
No one will hear the sound that it weaves
And my light will be blinded by the breathing air.

But the ants will bury it down beneath the land
So the rain won't be able to erase it,
And when they fall, the seeds will understand
And in their fruit the delicate worm will taste it.

Next year's light will bring new grass
That the sun will dry and turn into hay,
And with luck, a flock of drowsy lambs will pass
To graze on it some long and lazy day.

Then it will flow in their milk, starry and wise,
And no one will recall how it was brought
Into the world, conceived in sin, conceptualised
And made into words from thought.

I Only Need to Go to Sleep

I only need to go to sleep
To return to the place
That I alone believe I've departed,
Only myself, and the dogs
That feel me here as I come close
And fill this dream of tears with the yelps
Of their aggressive joy.
I only need to fall asleep
To notice the almost lascivious smell of green,
Of the high grass that brings on sleep,
The sleep within sleep,
Light that suffuses into light,
In the sensual and
All-knowing barks of the dogs,
At the edge of my lashes where
The landscape fades
And only your…

I Mustn't End

I mustn't end the
Gesture, my hand
Must not fill in
The circle it began.

Leave the transient
Fruit on the bough
And the taste we imagined,
Let it linger somehow;

May it never be complete,
I postpone, I wait;
The deed is old,
And ancient, the delight.

Only this desire
Is young beneath the sun –
I crave the perfumed scent
Until the perfume is undone.

I Do Not Sing the Leaf

I
Do not sing the leaf,
I only sing its tender death,
A death it hides in
Like an exhilarating country
That never ends,
And whoever goes there
Forgets to come back and dies
To be able to go on,
Always farther
And happier.
Only plants,
Because they cannot
Tell
What they see,
Are permitted to return
From that childlike country
From which
A mysterious catastrophe
Separates us
In vain.
I
Do not sing the leaf,
I only sing the tender death
It dreams of
Every year again.

The One Who Dreams Me

He may be trying
To redeem his soul this way,
My life is one of his lives
That he's condemned to dream
To purify himself
Of his sins,
I'm only a minor character
In this very odd
Ascesis
At the end of which he'll
Come to peace
And maybe grace.

Covered with Dew

Land of tender leaves,
Covered with dew,
How many thousands of years must pass
Before you tire of being born?
Cradle of misfortunes
So beautiful that no one
Has time to relinquish
Your verdant cemetery,
Earth rich with the salt
Of numberless tears
That riverbeds gather to
Fill their waters with fish
And your fertile sobs,
Restless mother
Tirelessly breeding
Sacrificial lambs,
You bring living grass from the dead
And from suffering, love.
Peace and quiet be with you,
Munificent provider,
Beneath a sky of forgotten blood,
Livid with cold, good night.

We've Learnt How to Laugh

We've learnt how to laugh
As though we were learning how
To handle guns.
The lucky ones only laugh in their dreams,
The unfortunate laugh all day,
We've been laughing for centuries
And no one understands,
And even we ourselves seldom understand
The ceaseless machine-gun fire of belly laughs
That keep us alive
Beneath the dim light of the moon,
As precisely as manacles.

In the Village I'm Going Back to

In the village I'm going back to
There are cuckoo clocks that shatter time to bits,
And giant chunks of silence
Lie scattered along the dusty roads.
The hands of the clocks spin crazily around
Pointing at something that nobody sees.
Long ago the hours fell off
And died,
But the hands keep running
And at times, confused,
The cuckoo pops out and announces
The end of the world, in a ditty.

A Church Filled with Butterflies

A church filled with butterflies
And icons coated with pollen,
Muffled in an eerie silence that
The whispering flutter of wings
Deeply and rhythmically poisons;
A church in which
Their bending
Antennae
Blindly grope the altar,
While the broken light
Pours onto the ambiguous rustling of
The robes of the saints
And the wings…
Sitting rigid in the pew
Trapped with horror in the midst of
Circling butterflies
I understand why it all seems familiar –
Those clumsy drawings of butterfly wings
I made when I was a child
And I learned to write,
I drew the church much later,
Unaware,
On the same piece of paper.

This Floating

What is happiness
If not this floating
Among the fruit and the leaves
In a shaft of dusty, honey-coloured light
In the enchanted place where life ends
But death does not begin,
And between the two there's only
A limpid craving
With the smell of fermenting plums
Or smoke and dried grass?
What is happiness
If not to fall asleep
Waiting for the end
In September
In an orchard?

Anchor

I suddenly remembered
How, in other times,
My gestures ended in my hands,
My smile reached my lips,
My vision stopped
In my cool, collected eyes.
Where is my body?
Has it waited for me
Awake in some unknown place
For centuries?
How many times have I passed it by, and looked,
Not knowing who it was?
I miss it.
The mouth that whispers 'I'm lonely'
With a soft, childish voice
In that tender anchor
Lying on the ground
To which I could return
And wake up
From time to time.

When I'm Living

When I'm living in my dream
In the world I'm dead
So am I dead in the beyond
When I'm still here instead?

Or is it only a game
With a moon and a sun
That share me sadistically
Controlling who I am?

When it's morning in my dream
It's nighttime on the earth
And I come back unwilling
From dream and living both.

I Come Back to Autumn

I come back to autumn as I come back home
From distant, freer and richer lands –
I know the coming winter, fog on the loam
And the endless mist that no one understands.

But I dream of afternoon's embrace in
The cold of night or day, the honey-sweet
Hour, the amber snow suspended in laces
From the conquered boughs of the apple tree.

I weep with joy in the fading glow
Of countless twilights, just before night,
And guilty grapes are crushed and overflow
For being too good, too sweet, too ripe.

I go towards the cold, though it makes me swoon,
Towards the fruit that ages and ferments
Into the limpid alcohol of noon
And grows translucent in the evening mist.

I'm afraid of the dark, yet I never fail
To come back from summer and sun-lit skies,
Where I yearn to suffer the happy ordeal
Of the grape that settles into wine and dies.

Sweet vanity and childhood love, the sum
Of fatal, drowsy dignity. With open hands
I come back to autumn as I come back home
From distant, richer and freer lands.

Early Gathered Grass

Smooth hills of early gathered grass.
Tall palaces of hay
From whose peaks
I used to slide and tumble
In a dizzying cataclysm
Of grass, of grass,
That set off the buzzing
And the savage scent
Of storms of bees
And warm snows of butterflies.
We never did finish
Before the sun
Disappeared behind the meek
Closed eyelids of the horizon
And a gentle voice whispered
'God is getting sleepy.'

Monastery of Wind

Could aroma be
A fortress of the air
With secret, hidden entrances
And glorious banners everywhere,
Built as lightly
On a stack
Of hay
As on a rotting corpse?
Monastery of wind,
All-powerful,
Unseen by eyes,
Revealed by smell,
A monastery fashioned
Of repugnance
Or caresses?
Scorned by time,
Unknown by place,
Fragile edifice
Of earth and breathing atmosphere
In strict proportions –
Haunted by a spirit,
Toppled by a puff of air...

Sea

Stop your crying, sea,
Stop crying, sea
Made pregnant by the waters of exasperated streams,
Cease your sobs,
The sky gone mad
From the prayers poured into him
Is father to the child
You will bear in sin.
You'll give birth to another sea,
A sea I could hardly dare
To look at, so end
Your crying, from which
Blackened clouds descend on the world
And birds with rain-heavy wings
Are unable to rise.
Butterflies turn back into worms,
Fruits go back to seeds,
Beasts and timid fish
Return, and die.
So stop this hysterical sobbing
And let us drink in silence here
The deep liquid darkness ebbing
From one of your tears.

It's So Cold

It's so cold here it freezes
The spittle on the teeth of dogs
While they howl at the moon
That drove them mad,
It's so cold and terrifying here
My lips split open when I cry
And I lick off the still-warm
Blood like a beast.

Sunday

Do you think I don't know
That behind
This magical flaming
Of the forest fallen into red
Is only that coward
Time passing by
And hiding its departure
With spectacular, hypocritical wonders?

You think I don't know
That quinces
Don't fall from
Their own regal weight,
But are defeated by caterpillars
Born of the cautious
Love
Of petty, mad and
Outlandish butterflies?

You think I don't know
That the victorious return
Of martins
Is only the result of
A cruel choice
By the evil and strong
Over the weak and good?

Don't worry,
They've told me
Everything and not a single delusion
Remains,
The masters have done their duty.

If the world seems perfect
On this Sunday afternoon
In autumn,
Only I'm to blame,
Only I will pay the price on Monday.

At the Mill Pond

The water of the mill pond glitters where
A viscid coat of emerald silk has formed
And the motionless, deserted wheels have grown
Green fur to soften them and keep them warm.

If you want to cross over, long hands cling to your boat
And heavy green stenches clog your lungs like lead,
While hidden frogs chant a solemn requiem
On this ageing, desecrated altar of bread.

Almost a century past, I looked on
Spellbound, as children frolicked there covered
In flour like snow, and among them I chose one,
In white, who would grow up to be my mother…

City of the Eastern Plain

City of the eastern plain
With sap exuding through your streets,
And an insolent sun that
Absorbs its festering prey in heat.

Melted city, river in flames,
And fierce aromas rising
To the sky, from fruit in which
The final thought will putrefy.

In the Country's Soul

In the country's soul
It's always yesterday,
The same old fears that it might not rain
Or there might be too much rain,
Garden hanging
On the forgetful floating of the clouds
And the absent-minded wind.
I dig up a grave
And read in the viscera of birds
What will happen
In the next two thousand years –
Wars begun by others
That we fight in heroically,
Silent and distracted,
Watching the clouds
The earth is hanging from.

Lascivious Fruit

Open, lascivious fruit, revealing
Its naked pit to the eyes,
And in the distant air, dazed
Vapours of alcohol rise.

Vegetal aromas of love
Beneath the sun of a sweltering day
Where golden plants emerge to
Sleep a summer long and pass away.

Indolence, drowsy and deep,
Even the bees are quiet in the wood,
This brilliant light so strong it
Fuses the river and the good

Into a blessing amazed
By its own munificence;
Sensual fruit with worms in flesh
That's sweet for so much shame…

In My Sleep

Sometimes, in my sleep
I happen to scream,
Only in my sleep,
And frightened by my own audacity
I wake up,
And I listen,
In the disciplined calm of night, for
Screams in my neighbours' sleep.
But wise neighbours only scream
When they're sure
That they dream they're asleep,
In a sleep within sleep
Where no one can hear them
And they can say whatever they want.
What freedom to make a racket
There must be there
In a sleep within sleep.

Lovers

And will we, in eternity, remain
As young as we are today, and bright,
When death beats in the tower of the brain
And closes red lids over ashen eyes?

Will we still in death be so easy to defeat,
And even then not understand
The meaning of that devastating word, repeatedly
Spinning its absurd commands?

Always young and beautiful and kind,
Always shyly glancing at each other's face,
Always sacrificed on other shrines
Homeless, and always out of place?

Lean on my arm when I have died*
And let yourself be broken by their
Ancient law. In return we've been requited
With the fortune of being a loving pair.

---

* This last stanza is inscribed on the tombstone of Ana Blandiana's husband,
Romulus Rusan. [Tr.].

Why?

Why does fruit have dreams of alcohol
And grass of warm and acrid scents
In a light so beautiful it prompts
Us to depart with gentle hints?

Why do clumsy cranes get startled
And hurriedly try to flee,
When they could wait in peace and
Disperse like clouds, more gracefully?

Why do cautious flowers take shelter
In seeds and bees retreat into hives,
When the autumn is so kind and good
And teaches us how to die?

To Stay Here in the Hay

To stay here in the hay and wait for night
While the light fades slowly from the sky,
And grumpy bumblebees get caught in your hair,
And every thought becomes a poetic line;

When the stars begin to shine like eyes
That glitter with curiosity,
To glide along on the smell of the grass
Like a swirl of air gliding out to sea;

And as you endlessly fall into sleep,
To dream the moon will wrap you in embrace
And its cold lips softly touch your flesh
And their traces will never be erased.

Drawing in Pastel

My country forsaken by fruit,
Forsaken by leaves,
Forsaken by grapes that
Have emigrated cautiously to wine,
My country betrayed by birds
Rushing and tumbling
In the astonished and still-clear sky.

Always at peace
With the scent of grass
That dies in the gentle sun,
Faithful spiders
Weave white cloths
To bandage
The leaf where the fissure has begun.

The dark night ripens your stars
And they ferment the sky,
A strong, bitter wind
Pushes on the day,
Falling walnuts
Measure your hours
And the quince shines down
On you respectfully.

Hamlet

More smell
Than sight or sound,
The smell of smoke on late afternoons
When drowsy herds come home
From drinking too much milk in the grass;
The smell of foaming milk
Squeezed sensually from udders, as if
The green soul of the grass
Suffused its milk-blue flesh
As wild and soft as
The breath of the smoke;
The smell of moistened straw
And piles of grain,
Of pyramids of wheat that reach the sky,
While the air of evening settles in
And clouds drift slowly into
Fading stories, and die;
The smell of yourself,
Hair warmed by the sun,
Dreams of grass and pastures in the skin
Dreams of sleep, and of the word –
Oh hamlet, built of eternal faith
In the air,
Loved by the breath
And shaken by the wind!

Alone with Myself

Alone with myself
And happy
Beneath the final sunlight in
The orchard, almost gone.
I can still hear the colours
Flowing through the leaves
And the faint crackle
Of fragile clouds.
Alone with myself.
Alone, all alone.
This gentle peace.
With nothing to tell myself.

Leaves of Animals

Leaves of animals wet in the rain shed
On shadows with fuzzy skin, arrayed
In a juicy sky that bends above your head
For you to take in and obey.

Wise golden noggins, hanging from the boughs
And thinking of scents to subject your will
To the temptress that rises softly now
Through the open, criss-crossing branches they fill.

And a murmur in the sensual leaves,
Promises and heresies whispered there
While the hour, as it gently flees,
Drips meaning into the breathing air.

A perfumed death is brewing in the quince!
How else would you ever wish to look?
Alone, with pious gestures, you make a defence
Of its golden rotting sphere among the books.

I Think Clouds*

I think clouds must tell different
Stories in different lands,
Maybe there are places where
People can see epics in the sky –
In our country flocks cross over the heavenly vault
With ageing dogs and melancholy lambs
Followed by a trio of shepherds
In the azure meadow.
Or, as in a dream,
An unearthly monastery rises
To be shattered in the merciless chaos
By the breath of a wind
And to rebel in heaven again
Until wings made of tiles
Fly upwards in fear
From the tears of a word.
How could we wish for
A clear sky and an empty dome above
When the clouds tell stories
That save us for eternity?
Batter us, storms
And make us flourish, pain
As long as you can write with sacred
Vapours on the ceiling of the world…

---

* This poem refers to two foundational anonymous ballads of Romanian literature, 'Miorița' and 'Master Manole', mentioned in the Introduction, see pp. 30-31. [Tr.].

A Vase with Wild Daisies

A vase with wild daisies
On a white desk
Where I write and am
Freer than I am;
Around me
The smell of hay
Allures me to a sleep
From which a word
May drip;
Sweet sky at sunset
Like the flocks of sheep
That used to come home;
Love for everything that was,
For everything that will disappear,
Love without meaning,
Love without frontiers –
Shadows of poplars, fence posts round the field,
Wild daisies
In a vase.

Country of Birds

A country is also made of birds
Flying south in a V,*
Wounded, chased away by the cold
And by treason,
To return
Humiliated by a yearning for home,
Gliding on the toboggan of the sky,
Thankful
That the eave is still attached
To the same old porch.
A country is also made of birds
Just as a church is also
Made of the hereafter.

---

* This image refers to the way birds fly in the sky in a V shape. Indirectly the poem alludes to those Romanians who, due to lack of freedom, defected to the West and were considered traitors by the communist regime. [Tr.]

Who Said It Was Gold

Who said it was
Gold,
This colour of
The ecstasy of leaves,
This triumphant
No-man's-land
Between life and death,
This bliss
That embraces the world
In its vegetal light
And the scent of naked
Fruit on the boughs
In virginal and
Heavy indecency?
Who could dare
To name
The most limpid
And profound eternity
Towards which
All of us flow,
Unworthy of so much hope,
Among clusters of sagacious grapes
And frenetic slender stems?
Be quiet!
Be quiet and listen to
The syllables of the grass, crackling
In the light's dry flame –
Not even the light would dare
To call this ultimate kingdom
By its name.

Poplars and Maples

Poplars and maples
Growing in a land
Unknown to others,
Where the clouds descend
And leafy branches rise,
Where the smallest doubt is able
To rock the dome,
Poplars and maples,
The slender angels
Of a verdant paradise.

Beat from time to time
Your shimmering wings
With emerald leafy veins
And hear how cuckoos sing
The time unceasingly,
As though a clock concealed
Somewhere deep beneath their feathers
Chimed
The hour
Of those that were deafened by eternity,

Eternity like a
Much louder death,
Deprived of silence
And the sweet anticipation without breath
Among the weeds of the burial place,
Peacefully ravel your unspun wool
And encircle the land
With words that
Only you and I can understand.

When I Grow Old Enough

When I grow old enough not
To want to die, I'll retreat
Into a silo, filled with
The restful smells of wheat

Beneath a dome of glowing reeds,
Of dried sunflowers and hay,
Of old, old dust in the air
That I remember from other days;

I'll lie down there on the heaps,
No wishes, no thoughts, no cares,
Not even words that glide
Through my dreams in pairs;

In that sweet coffin of grain
I'll close my eyes and smile,
And a beam of light from the roof above
Will play across my eyelids for a while;

Strangely drowsy and dazed,
From time to time I'll fall asleep,
Only to be roused from time to time
By the stumbling buzz of a bee,

And soon the aromas floating in the air
Will dissolve me down to the core,
I'll be older then, and contented,
And I will not want to die any more.

The Morning after Death

The morning after death will be
As cool as a misty September dawn.
Feeling lustful from the scorching summer heat,
I'll come to my senses in the white air,
Far from braided orchards in woolly light.
I'll get up early, as in September,
And, as in September,
I'll be all alone and able to hear
The air that drips through the day
On the quinces' moistened cheeks.
I'll be sleepy
And I'll pray to go to sleep again,
Just a little more,
Keeping myself still, my eyes
Closed and my face in the pillow,
While the deafening silence
Will wake me more and more
To begin, as on an autumn morning,
The eternal day.

THE CRICKET'S EYE

(1981)

In Sleep

Crickets only sing in their sleep,
In daylight they're only bugs at play,
Cover them, grass, to sleep untouched
By the suspicious sincerities of day.

May the translucent Lord of the dew protect
Them from dry and useless truth, and keep
Them safe, so everything they'll never live
Will visit them, at least, in their sleep.

Lull them into slumber, tied to their nightmare dreams,
The ropes like singing strings, their piercing tune
An offering made by delicate, dozing
Princes to the loneliness of the moon.

From Over There

From over there, from the leaf,
Someone is watching me,
With patience divided into summers and falls,
In silence,
And wondering why
My eyes are closed to him.

Oh, the grass grew over my lids
While they've been closed,
It was green and dry,
My eyelashes are stuck,
All knotted together,
And I can only see myself
Since his gaze
From the leaf has bathed me
In a green light, as though
I were preparing myself in
The depths of an everlasting ocean of patience
Without a word,
For harsher and longer resurrections.

As If

As if the light itself
Were a growing plant
And the stars had roots,
Thin, absorbing rays,
I can feel how they
Suck their inexplicable food
From my body,
All the stars following the scalpel
Like a flock of crows behind a plough.
I'm afraid of so much light,
I'm too cold for so many flowers,
I'm sleepy with so much love
And I don't know whom to call on
To put out this heavenly
Garden of light inside of me,
To break through
This ecstatic dam
In the ocean of darkness.

Egg

Do you remember how good
It was, enclosed forever in
The egg on the waters
Where the universe fits,
A single being, complete inside
And all self-sufficient,
Light afloat on light?

Do you remember how we floated there?
Love with no yearning
Only reflecting itself, speechless
And content, like a spring,
Pain hadn't yet been invented,
Loneliness didn't exist.
The word was not yet born.

Who was to blame? When did it end?
The perfect egg was split in two,
It broke into heaven and earth
And suddenly the world grew lonely –
Do you remember how new it had all become –
When the blade passed between us
Reinventing us, one by one?

Do you remember how the cells
Divided themselves and the terror
Of blood that wanted to flow
Through a single body?
The earth reached up into the trees
And the sky was tangled in branches
To cover the naked wound
Where they had broken in two.

Do you remember what was wasted,
The feelings and words,
The animals and plants
Running to the same lost shore
And waiting for the end of the world
From which, perhaps, a perfect egg
Will be born, floating on the waters
In the silence of the beginning.

The Land Where Parents Lived

My hair had grown down to the ground
And thirty years old
Seemed so far away
That I hardly imagined
I'd reach that age some day.
Without a thought, I eagerly went
From the land where my parents lived
To a world I had yet to invent.

Even today that world is not invented.
My hair isn't long any more.
Thirty was only a stop for food on a road that hasn't ended.
Oh what I'd give to be back where my parents were!

But we always get there late –
The land where parents lived,
When everyone has gone.
And in the moonlight
Under the chestnut trees
Now cut down
Only the shadows remain
Of fathers condemned
And mothers, thirty years old,
Who comb
Their daughters' hair,
So long it reached the ground.

Behold

Behold, I bathe in a river made of seconds
And towel myself with a cloth of hours,
And for many years
I've combed my hair in a mirror of time,
And the blade of grass is a season of green,
And the stalk of hay is a season of dry,
And the sky is a weather that slips away
With no frontiers;
For time is never the core,
But only the beginning and the end –
And death is also a span of time
Until you are dead
And then, unborn from the hands of the clock,
The river abides in itself
Like a sea.*

---

* Allusion to the poem 'The First Letter'(1881) by the Romanian romantic poet Mihai Eminescu, 'Dead time extends its body and transforms itself into eternity.' [Tr.]

I'm Tired

I'm tired of being born of the Idea,
I'm tired of not being able to die –
I've chosen a leaf,
From this leaf I'll be born, after
Its image and likeness, cool
Sap running slowly through the veins
To form my fragile bones;
From it I'll learn to tremble, to grow,
And the pain will make me shine,
Then I'll fall from the bough
Like a word from a mouth.
The childish way
You die
When you're
A leaf.

Definition

This house woven of willowy boughs
And sculpted like Adam from clay,
This house covered with an organ of reeds
And ready to burst into melody;

Washed in the dew and drenched in the sun,
Wrapped like a little god in a cloud
And drawn, like the sea, to the moon at night
With your porch and its crickets chirping loud;

This house protected by trees and vines
Watched over by fireflies and bees that hum,
On which pumpkins boldly climb and
Pummelled by branches heavy with plums;

Constructed of letters and pillars of
Syllables set into words, hung from the stars,
Silence surrounds you with white empty sheets
And the sky rains ink on what you are.

Metamorphosis

The angels have put on clothes of a bird
That pinch them beneath their wings.
The birds have put on clothes of a fish
To fly beneath the sea in herds.
Grass is growing in the armpits of beasts
And subtle roots in their hooves,
And words in love are mating
To bring forth new insulting words.
As if it weren't I
Who's calling out
For help,
I cover my ears so as not to hear
And my eyes grow
Heavy, like millstones,
With a groan.
I'm like
A buried seed
That doesn't want to be –
Neither plant, nor earth.

Boat

I'll weave a boat of flowers and grass
To float out among the reedy isles
Halfway between the river's banks and
Far from where the fishes pass,
Stars will redeem me in the night, and dawn
Surround me with golden swirls of stream
Like a stepmother's staring eyes.

Lulled by the motion of the sleepy waves,
Eyes half closed, I'll only perceive a deep red
Nothingness, filled with stars, and my death
Will be filled with dreams, left to be
Answered too late.

Late, the boat of woven grass is rocking.
Greenish, salt-scented airs will embrace me.
Tangled with snakes and undulating weeds,
I'll set into the empty sea
And I won't remember a thing.

Crossings

From one end of sleep to the other
I feel that I'm in danger
At those hazardous crossings
Clumsily placed between lives,
Boats that don't connect to form a bridge
Across a swirling river
That wants to keep them apart,
I slowly and carefully fall asleep
So as not to step on death
And I'm especially scared to wake up,
When I could slip
Into a foreign life, estranged,
From which I couldn't come back
And where everything here is to blame.

At Daybreak

At daybreak,
When the nighttime air
Steals softly away
To the hemisphere of longing,
The tiny chalice of the flower
Opens to the light
With a deep and vibrating
Sound, like the moan of a cathedral dome
That echoes with a clang of deafening bells.
It's a pity our ears
Can't hear it
And that no one ever knows
For whom the bells
Of the flowers toll.

Hymn

You come from where my eyes can't see
And you grow to where my sight can't reach,
A leafy bridge above ruin and loss,
The raw material of the cross.

Fragile column holding up the sky,
The fruit of both evil and good,
The sap of truth in you never runs dry
And the serpent encircles your body of wood.

Inverted meaning of the worlds we can see
With roots growing into the breathing air
And leaves like curious rafts that will bear
A soul on the river of death with ease.

Greatest fatherhood of the earth,
Immaculate motherhood of birth,
Make me rustle in each breath of wind
And teach me how to die again.

Clothing

Sometimes, in the morning
I wake up freezing cold
And, still half asleep,
Drowsy and shivering, I put on
My youthful body,
Warm and silky,
My teeth chattering like a child,
Happy that another day,
For one whole day,
I'll be
Sheltered from eternity.

Wonder

The wonder crackles beneath my feet,
Barely dressed in the
Form of wet branches,
It trembles overhead
And drips on me,
Its voice is crystal clear
And incomprehensible.
It flows over stones and
Makes them beautiful,
It drowses in the berries
And ripens them as they sleep.
The pine cone is its palace
And the eye of the mole its swing;
Every tree is
A candle.
It holds everything:
Fruit and roots,
Bees and butterflies,
Evil and good
In heaven and on earth.
It even holds me,
Unworthy,
Never expelled
From the paradise
I almost profaned
By trying
To understand.

Inside a Walnut

Braided with blades of grass
And sealed with leaves
My chains will soon be dry
And all fall off.
I'll be so free
That I'll be cold
And who and what
Can teach me?

Who has ever been inside a walnut
And can show me the cells
Where I can lock myself away,
When the whole universe
Is nothing more than a chamber
Dimly lit by quince?

There are four rooms in a walnut, hot
And dark, with the sweet smell at the core,
Only a curious cricket can see inside –
I wish I could grow into autumn in a walnut

And be covered by layers of leaves
And the shadows of flocks
Of birds, itching to depart,
While I, with all the luck in the world,
Know well how to choose
And soundly sleep in a walnut.

Icons on Glass*

Mounted on a sorrel horse – light brown,
Saint George gallops bravely above my bed,
A broken halo and crooked spear thrust down
Into the dragon's mouth. Its scales are like tin.
Its tongue is red.

The sky is green; the beard on the saint looks wiry.
The dragon too, poor thing, has a beard of greenish hairs.
The horse looks surprised; its eye makes an enquiry:
What should it do with its golden hoof in the air?

What could I teach it? Should I speak or laugh?
The saint's heavy head seems ready to tumble to earth.
I pity that ugly beast with a gadfly's wings of glass,
And the innocent horse, tethered up there to belief.

---

* Painting icons on glass is a Romanian folk art that emerged in Transylvania
in the 17th and 18th centuries and is characterised by a naïve, richly coloured
drawing but without anatomical proportions or perspective. [Tr.]

Hibernation

Don't listen to my brothers, they're fast asleep,
They don't understand the words shouted out
While they howl like complacent beasts
With souls that dream of beehives
As they swim among seeds.

Don't hate my brothers, they're fast asleep,
They've covered themselves with a bearskin
That keeps them implacable and cruel and alone
In this senseless cold
That had no end.

Don't judge my brothers, they're fast asleep,
At times, one may be obliged to wake up
And, if he doesn't go back it means he's dead,
And it's night and it's cold
And the sleep goes on.

Don't forget my brothers, they're fast asleep
And while they sleep they give birth and the children grow
And they imagine that life is sleep, and they
Can hardly wait, impatient, to wake up
Into death.

Flight

No one dies of the disease
I'm suffering from;
But one lives –
Its substance is eternity itself,
A kind of cancer of time
That grows and grows unceasingly.
A perfect disease,
An endless suffering like a vowel of glass
Ringing through the deafening air,
A falling that,
Precisely because it never ends,
Is called a flight.

Loneliness

Loneliness is a city
Where everyone else has died.
The streets are clean.
The squares are deserted
And everything suddenly seems
To be so much bigger in that
Neatly fated void.
Loneliness is a city
Where it snows and snows
And not one footprint
Mars the light
That settles in layers
And only you, your watchful eye
Alert above the sleepers,
Observe and understand, and you never get tired
Of so much silence, so much flawlessness
Where no one fights
Or is deceived,
Where even the tear of an abandoned animal
Is too pure
To be able to hurt any more.
In the valley
Between suffering and death,
Loneliness is a city of contentment.

Half of the Moon

Half of the moon falls
Awkward through the night –
Angel of solitude,
Make me forget,

Make me forget, or
Make me go to sleep
In this loneliness growing
Deformed and deep.

And, wise angel, if I
Should dream, then make
Me not recall
When I awake.

Make me forget
Or make me write,
Desolate angel,
With continual cries.

My cold eye, angel,
Cover it I plead
With an eyelid
That can bleed on

The things we see
Too lucidly.
Lie to me gently and
Lead me to believe,

Give me the unknown
Half of the moon,
But make me forget,
Oh, angel of doom.

Destroy this delirium
Of memories forced
So my loneliness won't
Surprise me any more.

Otherwise

What if the sun and the moon
Are one and the same star
That the fear of the dark
Disguises as two different things?
What if I'm only a being
Blinking beneath your blue eye
Or scratching at a foreign
Granite dome with my gaze?

The same poor clothing of the flesh
Designed to dress the same
Great fear, though different,
Always running from something else,
The same river always flowing,
Always giving voice to other muddy banks –
From which one same longing
Pours, unchanged, into the sea.

Inhabited by a Song

It isn't my song,
It only passes through me at times,
Incomprehensible and uncontrollable,
It clothes me easily
Like the gods of antiquity
Who walked among humans
Dressed in a cloud.

I don't know when it comes,
I don't know when it goes,
Nor where it is
When it's not in me.
This is my lot, to wait for
The indulgence of the alien moment.

Inhabited by a song,
Abandoned by a song,
Maybe even the widow of an
Unknown but beloved song,
I don't deserve your laurels
Except for the humility
Of having kept faithful to it
Endlessly.

In the Water

I look at the water,
I forget myself in the water.

Sitting on this grassy bank
And looking into the water
I contemplate my flowing face,
A stranger,
Wrinkled by storms,
Made rough by the wind and
Aged by the passing of waters
That never return.

Sitting on a riverbank
Woven with enchanted grass,
Enchanted weeds and flowers
That draw their forgetful youth from the river
And it isn't enough for me to exist,
I want to see myself
Reflected in
The curling page
Of the wave.

Nighttime on a Bed of Hay

Nighttime on a bed of hay,
Stars in the sky and plums in
The trees, I could stay
For lives and deaths on end

Within this cradling quiet
Slowly woven by a cricket
Exiled from the moon
Deep into my mind;

These sharp perfumes and smells
That I had long forgotten –
Let me stay here, thankful
Just to wait and listen,

As if I didn't recognise
Myself completely,
Enchanted by my cries
Like an unfamiliar melody,

As if I didn't know
Myself, or comprehend.
I could stay here alone
For lives and deaths on end.

The Step

I decided
To leave my voice, like
Leaving a church abandoned
By God,
A famous church
Turned into a museum,
Whose altars are syllables
And vaults are words,
Beneath which, overwhelmed
By so much love,
The faithful crowd into
The sacred vestibule.

I decided
To escape my voice
As though it were a prison
I had built myself
For my countless crimes,
A famous prison
Turned into a museum
With locks made of verses
And bars made of rhymes –
The public visit it
And, appalled by the torture,
Aren't surprised
That nothing lies inside.

One, Two, Three

Plums fall – one, two, three,
First through the blue, then to the hell of green.
Into the sky, into the grass,
First with birds, and then with snakes at last.
No power can make them stay from
Falling along their solemn way.
And when they arrive, naked and sweet,
They softly lay their heads, and breathe,
On a cushion of alfalfa leaves
And there they very patiently wait
To ferment into alcohol.
Then one by one, the kernels go down
Deeper and deeper into the ground
To reach, through greater pain,
A future life to come.
How simple and certain
The death of a plum!
Its afterlife is spring.

The Line

Words cross the street
Like a line of orphans
From the Children's Home,
Each with a fist stuck
Into the coat of the one in front,
Their only concern is
Not to be separated
One from the other.

The Name

How foreign my own name sounds in my ears,
Nobody else has a name like mine,
I don't understand who allowed it to choose me,
Or how I let myself be locked inside.

A clumsy story – I'll disappear
And this usurper will stay in my place,
This word that has no meaning for me
Whose meaning is me, when I've been erased.

A song repeated awkwardly in fragments
Sung to the drumbeat of others, and a
Song that I wait for, always surprising
Like a feminine rhyme, with ana.

A whole life given for a life hereafter,
A tiring life, and misunderstood, tied
To a crushing and futile destiny,
My only right, to assume it with pride.

But among the seeds and grass, the worms and bees
I can't help having a name they append
That I can't distinguish from the noise
And commotion that hem me in.

Everything spins and flows and sings
Triumphant laws I can never defy,
Against which I can only try to sleep
To dream of the name I know myself by.

I'm So Cold

I'm so cold
That I think
I could only save myself
Like those freezing men
They used to sew
Into the bellies of animals
To warm them up
And so, bundled
Into a robe of painful pelt and
Smeared with the blood of beasts,
They came to life again.
Too far from
The flames of hell,
I was frozen by my
Angelical loneliness,
But who will be able
To open his ribcage
To take me in?

Armour

This body
Is no more than the armour
That an archangel
Chose to wear to pass through the world
And, disguised like this,
With its wings wrapped up
Inside of me,
With the visor of its smile
Hermetically sealed on my face,
It goes into the heat of battle,
Is assaulted by injury and insult,
Soiled by vicious looks
And even caressed
On the steel plating of its skin
Beneath which revulsion incubates
An exterminating angel.

One More Step

So few things I know how to do,
No peaches like peach trees,
No grapes like vines,
Not even nuts
Like the walnut tree with its bitter shade
And soft rustling leaves,
One thing I can do
With extraordinary skill:
I know how to die.

It's not a boast,
I know how to die like few people do –
First I wrap myself in silence,
Then I slowly advance into
The void, one step, another step,
And one more step,
Until all that's left to see
Is a voice,
Sumptuously seated in
The coffin of a book.

It's not a boast,
Believe me, I know I'm going to die
And I know, above all, I'll be resurrected,
But that, of course,
Will be much easier.

A Game

See how the rain sews
The earth to the sky like a hem.
Its silken threads go
Back and forth in the wind.

See how the grass weaves
A landscape in the clouds.
I've always believed
And I say out loud:

From where you can see
The grass looks like rain
That falls on the green
Sky's inverted plain,

And a greyer grass
Will rain down in sheets
On the cloudy pathway
Beneath your feet.

Now let's change, so
You can see my way –
You give me a halo,
I'll give you a name;

And should anyone ask us
If they're both the same –
The cloud-rain is grass
And the sky-grass is rain;

But we both want to know
The reason, the why –
The cloud-rain grows and
The grass splashes up to the sky.

The Hunt

I've never hunted for words,
I've only searched for their long
Silver shadows,
Drawn across the grass by the sun,
Pushed across the sea by the moon.
I've never hunted for anything more
Than the shadows of words:
An ingenious hunt
Learnt from the old ones
Who know
That its shadow is the most valuable
Part of a word
And that words that have no shadows any more,
Have sold their souls.

Shadow

Whoever walks forward
And doesn't look back
Has left himself behind;
Whoever runs
Is running in fear
To avoid being caught
By himself;
Whoever doesn't acknowledge his goal
Is afraid
He won't find
Himself there,
As though a shadow
Weren't the puddle of darkness itself,
That drains from our open veins
Because we wish to move forward…

Pathway

Straight pathway
Traced through the grass
By the comb of my bare feet,
As though it were the hair
Of the earth,
Its head warm with sleep,
Ready and willing to
Collapse in the fall,
Like the aged, in the autumn of life.

One Day

One day, someone will have to come,
Someone from death's farther side,
One day someone will tell me
What the far away hides.
One day, I'm sure, they'll teach me
How to act, transferred
To the northern side of words.
When I'm called, I'll have to know
What to say, long before I go
And what to do when I escape,
For they cannot force
Me to a new initiation,
Make me start it all again
With no preparation.

Proof

Angels beaten with stones
Who still have the strength
Not to fly away through the air,
Wounded and exhausted,
Ask me for shelter.
Humble and fragile, they fall asleep, softly
Rustling their wings among my notebooks.
And if they get cold
Before they sleep,
I place a white sheet on their wings.
Next morning, the wing prints on the pages
Prove that it wasn't a dream
And I hurry to memorise them
Before they're taken away
To be used to detect new species
Of birds of prey.

The Shadow of a Blade of Grass

The shadow of a blade of grass,
What could be more fragile
Than the shadow of the grass,
Than a thin line of darkness
In the threatening, invasive light,
What could be more heroic
Than the shadow of a blade of grass
Laboriously climbed by
The shadow of a ladybird,
Just as dark?
Long detached from the forms
They project against the light,
Existing pathetically
On a hot afternoon:
The shadow of a ladybird
Painfully climbing
The shadow of a blade of grass,
What could be more fragile,
More impossible to delete?

Semantics

I have to admit that I still haven't managed
To decipher the cricket's tongue,
Though I've been preparing for years
To do so.
I attended the prestigious universities
Of the month of August,
I wrote scholarly papers
On how the evening threshes the stars
And I obtained my PhD
On the loosely related dialect
Of the poplar leaf.

And all of that just to get into
The strident palace
Floating in the air on columns of vowels,
With long corridors of screams,
Dungeons of wails and laments
And towers shouting hallelujahs.

Sometimes I thought I was beginning to understand
The web of sharply vibrating sounds
And I rushed to set up systems,
Morphologies and puzzling
Syntaxes,
Until a shattering and uncontrollable
Cry broke through sense
And all the models collapsed.

Oh my, what languages of sounds I
Could have invented,
If only I hadn't listened to
The incomprehensible cricket.

Camouflage

What more could we ask of paradise
Than it be like
A swallow's nest?
On the inside
Immaculate and bright,
Lined with feathers
Like angels,
Lumpy clay
On the outside,
A perfect camouflage
For what we call
With so much precaution
Death.

In the Deep, Dull Thud

In the deep, dull thud of purple plums
On moistened earth at harvest time
Life and death, voluptuous and
Shameless, intertwine.

They bring both pleasure and pain:
The rot is sweet, and fulfilment ends –
In the deep, dull thud of purple plums
Life and death profoundly contend.

Equally triumphant, always chained
Together in love and war, cruel and
Brimming with the same inescapable song
In the deep, dull thud of purple plums.

Seed

With my hand all covered in earth,
Alone, I touch my cheek,
Dust leaves a mark on dust like
The first day, gentle and meek.

And I feel like a seed in the mud
That grows on my cheek, and soon
Sends amorous roots through my flesh,
Tingling in the light of noon.

I wouldn't be surprised if a flower
Bloomed with my blood flowing inside
Like a food that reached me from another
Earth, a land far away and wide.

Falling

First I throw out
The words, one
By one,
They drop down wisely,
Mating as they
Fall;
Then the years
Equally distant
One by one,
With a subtle knowledge of gradations;
Then, as on a sinking
Ship, I hurry to throw
Off the ballast,
Everything that can drag me down,
Memories, desires, passions,
Love, and finally,
When there's nothing left
To cast away,
Not even a coat, however thin,
I take off my wrinkled skin
And the numbed flesh from the bone.
This is the great striptease
I carry out
Almost willingly.

Moon Just Touching

The moon just touching the tower
Climbs to the cross at its peak,
The yellow of her sullen cheek is
Like a corpse, or a jaundiced flower.

Then she slowly and obliquely
Moves away, shedding her light
Across the vast expanse of night,
A Tibet of rooftops, sleeping meekly.

Her image glides, then hops from
Windowpane to windowpane
And barely trembling, glides again
Above our house, and stops.

I know she's waiting, wicked-seeming,
Patient, for me to come outside;
Her large eye hardly blinks. It hides
A mysterious meaning.

I pretend I'm not aware she's
Dripping into me, like rain,
The moment I had so much feared
That makes me feel ashamed.

Listening, I softly walk through the air;
I slowly undress, and wait:
The moon has long been dead. It's late.
The sky is too old to care.

Brush Pen

The winter boughs, all hushed,
Pen Japanese haiku with
A smoky writing brush
Across the silk of the snow,

As though they wanted me
Not to understand, lines shared
In vain, even though we all
Had sat and shed our tears*

Beneath the same trees
In the same century –
Angels, mute and clumsy,
Teach me to be wary.

Poems we can never know,
They drop down from the snow:
Yesterday they came too soon,
Today they're yesterday, and gone.

---

* Allusion to 'By the rivers of Babylon, there we sat down, yea, we wept, when we remembered Zion.' Psalm 137:1. [Tr.]

Earth

This body
That's wounded
Even by caresses,
With shoulders where wings
No longer try to grow,
Is the only strip of land
Where I can build
An earthly kingdom.
When I lose you
Feeble universe,
More transient than a leaf,
Tenuous empire of an hour
Guided by luck,
Will all of my armies of angels,
Playing at hide-and-seek,
Be able to take your place?

Question

What does the lamp feel for the moth,
What does the moon feel for the sea
And the sun for the earth,
The earth itself for the moon's round sphere,
The word for thought, its place of birth,
And the giant eye for prayer and plea
As it moves across the egg-white horizon
With a look that holds us together here?

Leaves and branches and flowers, but
Not one animal answering,
Not one living entity
Can give a definite yes,
Through an always random sky,
Though it isn't foreign enough,
We fall with folded wings
And never even ask.

Illumination

How big and bright
The seconds are here,
Their foreheads and shoulders are blinding –
What do they do
To avoid growing old
And dying?
Just rarely, from
Time to time,
And for no reason at all,
One of them decides at last
To slip into
The past.
Mother death, the seconds,
How great they are
Here among udders and ants,
Pumpkins and bees.
I can't find one that's
Foolish or kind-hearted enough
To have some pity
And let itself
Go out in me.

If

And if, in the surrounding night
I set myself on fire with a
Well-known gesture in the main square,
Would anyone be woken up
By the bright light or
Wonder where the smell
Of smoke was coming from?
A peace interrupted from time to
Time by the heat on the asphalt
That sensually cracks beneath the power
Of a fistful of grass. It smells
Like a blossoming tree in a yard
And you can almost hear the
Fruit grow from the flower.
History,
Weaker and more senseless than
An invisible thread of pollen,
From which a fruit is born…

---

* Allusion to Jan Palach, the Czech student who immolated himself in 1969
in Wenceslas Square in Prague as a form of political protest against the Soviet
invasion; over time, it also refers to Corneliu Babeș, who committed suicide by
setting himself on fire in Brașov in 1989 against Nicolae Ceaușescu's regime.

Morphology

A longing, almost gone, for the world,
A longing for myself, almost undone,
Nouns and pronouns swirl
In an unknown tongue

Within whose phrases,
Old and soft, like a velvet peach,
Verbs ferment the hazy
Idea of dreaming in my speech.

The only language I murmur
In my sleep, and my thought can save,
A tormented declension heard
Between cradle and grave;

The language the ocean understands
And even the mountains speak –
Sweet, inherent law of man,
Adjectives and conjunctions, the heat

Of burning interjections prepare
A thought that wants to come alive,
A longing for a world where
Parents still are and childhood thrives.

Thank You

Thank you for leaving me him,*
Stones whose soul I believe in,
And you, disaster, whose meaning
I've understood, thanks to you again.

Thank you for not taking him away,
Yellow eye in the forehead of the dead
Sky, voracious moon whose gaze
I feel on the back of my neck and head.

And you, screaming shards of icons,
Cutting halo, angelic raiment that bleeds,
You didn't bury him completely,
For which I give you my gratitude.

I'm sorry I haven't loved you till now,
Walls and beams, columns of the same dream,
Rivers of lava from the infirm belly of the earth
That didn't kill him then.

You could have done it. The ironic end
Of the world gave you that infinite right.
The silken eyelashes of the stars
Would not even have blinked at the sight.

---

* Ana Blandiana's husband was miraculously saved after falling from the seventh to the fourth floor in the earthquake (with a magnitude of 7.2 on the Richter scale) that struck Bucharest on 4 March 1977 and which killed 1,578 people and injured 11,300.

Mirrors

How hard it is to find,
And easy to create,
Thousands and thousands of regents
For the king that's passed away.

For just a single moon,
Thousands of lakes below;
I thirst to drink myself,
I drink only mirrors though.

Thousands of screaming words
For a dying sense;
I'm thirsty for sleep,
I'm sleepy for silence.

Pity

An owl barked
On our house last night
Like an abandoned dog
Alone among symbols,
A miserable cry,
Judging by the sound
It must have been desperate,
Lonely and hideous,
An owl
On our house.
Watching it
In the frightening starlight,
I didn't understand
The threat it made.
I only felt pity
And I wished the prophecy
Had been fulfilled
So that it, too, could be happy.

Words

Are they words, perhaps, what I say;
And if they are words, what is that?
Round surfaces of sound
Jagged with meaning,
Through which my thought can breathe
As a tree lives through its green
Leaves in the sky, pulsing with the
Destiny of hidden roots

Surrounded by earthworms and mud,
Fearfully embracing the dead,
To learn from speechless fate
Eternally overthrown
The rhythmic silence of the stem
That speaks through leaves and is born through blooms.
But if what I say are words,
Isn't it useless not to pass away?

Every Trace

Every trace is a wound,
Don't turn your head
And don't stare at
The swollen traces
You've left on things
And the wounds of your steps
Bleeding with mud.
Every trace is a wound
In the white flesh of failure,
Don't let your dream
Be twisted,
Avid for the suffering
Of the past.
Move on
Embalmed in oblivion,
Devoid of memories, like a dead man
Devoid of his rotting innards.

Nevertheless

And nevertheless, if we ever awake
From this harried sleep,
Will we then remember how, one day,
We died beneath the snow piled deep?

How earth was made a platinum sphere,
How hours fit towers and flakes fit the air?
Thought, astonished, falters still
Like the tongue of a bell under water.

There's too much white for eyes to stay
Open and so much peace in death and the world!
Were we really murdered on purpose that day
And was it, in fact, the snow as it swirled?

Postponement

Imagine that one evening
The sun will set completely
And you'll have to dream
In that final night
The countless dreams you've
Always postponed;
You'd have to hurry to dream
About falls down stairways with missing stairs
And unearthly voices
That mix the unbearable pain
Of betraying others with
The hardly noticed betrayal of yourself,
A placid treachery.
You'd have to hurry to dream
Emotions and events,
Loved ones and crimes,
Birds and snakes,
Voices, mountains, ships,
The depths of the sea and clouds,
Everything your soul had put off
For later,
For the incredible
Moment when
To the sarcastic sounds of bugles
You will enter the hereafter
Against all expectation
According to your dreams.

Home

There was a time when I felt
At home in my body,
I knew where everything was –
The window onto the sunrise
And the northern wall,
I never felt lonely,
I kept myself busy
From morning to night,
And whenever I went out
I was eager to return.

Now I'm tired of so much order
And knowing it all makes me sleepy,
I don't remember when I was brought
To this room that's too beautiful for me.
Was I searching for someone and came here and stayed?
Or was it, maybe, a trap that
Now I can't get out of?
I've been waiting a long time and I've forgotten for whom…
Oh, I feel so cold in this house!
If I left it now, it would be forever.

Wind, Unroll

Wind, unroll
The singular ball
Of gossamer,
Before I
Spin a word
Out of my time here,
Tie my hands
With the tearful strands
So I won't pass away
Beneath the sky
Like a bell of glass
On the moon,
In which I hang
And clumsily swing
And make a heavy sound
Every time I pound on
Heaven's walls and rafters,
To mark the time of the hereafter.

In Memoriam

How will the wind
Be able
To shake the stars
In autumn;
How will the autumn
Be able
To wilt the stars
In the sky;
How will the sky
Be able
To teeter
On the passing of time
And fall on its face;
How will time
Be able
To pass and
Pass forever?

Circle

I can't rejoice in the shining
Circle around my head,
At night in my dreams
I can hardly remember that wonderful shape
From when I used to play at rolling
It through the dust with a stick,
Running behind to keep up
And hitting it again
To make it roll
Once more.
It can't be seen in mirrors,
It can't be touched,
Only the startled eyes of others
Show me it's there –
With rays stuck into my skull
I'd make my head roll on the ground
If I knew my shoulders could see.

Eleusis

Everything ends with a sprig of wheat
That houses orgies
And reveals itself to the masses on the temple steps.
Oh, we could roll on
The cold slabs of stone struck by bodies
Still alive, still alive, and rapt
In turn with hatred and desire,
With love or with ire,
The same unbridled fight
That demands more than it expects,
When everyone knows that
Everything ends with a sprig of wheat…

Epitaph*

Sleep peacefully here,
In the smell of paper
Written on with pain
And hardly understood,
Delicate god of the temple
Called Childhood –
So many sacrifices offered
For so few sins.

Sleep peacefully here,
Buried in faint
Rhymes you can no
Longer hear, atoned
And fully holy but
Unlicensed saint
Among cowardly bishops
And cruel angels of stone.

Sleep peacefully here,
Dreaming a fate
For I know not how many Jobs
Who have risen to a new estate,
Who have passed through prisons
And gentle flames
To a paradise
Filled with sugar cane.

Sleep peacefully here,
Moved a second time. Stay warm.
May the earth be light above your form.

Over the Tops of Plum Trees

Over the tops of plum trees heavy with worms,
Over leafless vines and
Cornfields unharvested,
The waning moon
And silence broken by a train,
They pass by solemnly, ridiculous, like two
Empresses
Long dethroned,
Long ago dethroned,
Who still believe that empires
Tremble
And palaces rise
Beneath their gaze...
Loneliness woven of thistles, grass and leaves,
Satellites and stars entwined
In the same terrible sky
Churning above this brutal world,
The crimson tips of lonely
Metal angels' wings unfurled.

And yet, there still are crickets,
There still are leaves,
Bonfires of broken branches and hay,
Words unspoken,
Large birds of prey
And master over all, the relentless earth.

---

* **'Epitaph'** *(see opposite page)*:This is an autobiographical poem referring to
Ana Blandiana's father, Gheorghe Coman (1915-64), an Orthodox priest and
a political prisoner, who died shortly after his release from prison. His wife
buried him in Oradea, where he had served as a priest; but years later, at his
mother's wish, he was transferred to the Timişoara cemetery in the family plot.

I Breathe, I Breathe

I breathe, I breathe,
My eyes kept closed,
The sharp-edged stars write soft, keen
Signs on my eyes through their lids
Like dead fish floating on the water's sheen.
As though it were a dream – I breathe, I breathe,
The thick glass vault of heaven gleams and
Almost cracks when the stars' frozen blood
Swells out till it has to burst at the seams;
And then the light scrapes, long and slow,
Like gravel under a moving hoe,
And the sound of your footsteps recedes
Dull, like a chiming of bells beneath the sea
And the waves advance – coming closer and
Closer, so transparent they can't be seen;
As though it were a dream – I breathe, I breathe
The crystal that will come to bury me.

Vowel

Just as someone cut by a scalpel
Doesn't sing his pain,
As someone stabbed in the back
Has no time to versify
His indignation and death
And can only produce
A stifled A,
Superior in concentration
To the poems of the still-living world,
I could simply
Shout out a long, endless vowel,
Because I don't know
What poem has ever
Managed to penetrate
More deeply into
The bowels of suffering
Than the letter A.

How I Would've Wished

How I would've wished that
Everything were perfect, like
A plant that only slow, belated
Autumn could kill,
And on which the snow
Was lucky enough still
To fall in another life.

How I would've wished
That no one else had been like us,
Beautiful, pure and clean,
Never needing to fight,
That we had passed through the world
Protected from lies forever,
Marvelling at pain,
Happy to be together
In another life.

How I would've wished
We could always be the same,
Always young and sliding down a slope
At whose end, wet and deep,
The moon is reflected, a shimmering flame
In another life.

How I would've wished.
If we only could have missed
That one exalted moment of strife,
Just enough for hatred to splatter us
With death,
To split us farther and farther
Apart like a knife,
Alone and so old

That we wouldn't know each other,
Even if we came together
In another life.

Weave

Crucified in a spidery web,
And dying, I can still admire its weave –
No urge to escape from the fate
I've written for myself. Like hate
The poem has woven nets around itself
To capture signs and words.
This is my defeat: I myself am a word
Whose meaning I can't remember.

Reflection

The air is an ocean
Cloudy at times,
Sometimes clear,
But never quite transparent
Because beings
Living up there
On its beaches
Are able to see us,
Trapped in the mud of the depths
And to dive,
Holding their breath,
To where we are.
But, when they see us
Wouldn't they imagine
They see themselves
Reflected in the mire?

Instead of

Instead of the roaring seas
Sensually rocked by storms
And swollen by the moon,
Hiding splendours and disasters
In their depths,
I chose,
Putting it in the balance,
This drop of dew,
Trembling, precarious, on a leaf,
Within which the whole sun fits
Into the magnifying glass of our gaze,
I alone chose,
Happy and with no hope.

Olly Olly Oxen Free

My Lady of autumn, pardon if I ask;
Are you fond of rotted plums in the grass?

My Lady of dust, could you say to my face
How wet, round pips and kernels taste?

My Lady of weather, I'm curious, explain;
How do you like my cheek in the rain?

My Lady of death, I haven't heard;
Are you comfortable swallowing bitter words?

My Lady of eternity, you've never told;
How do you feel about my soul?

My Lady of rebirth, can you say if, or when
We'll start all over again?

And most of all, how many times you'll bring
Us back, my young Miss spring?

Feverish Planet

Feverish planet explored by a cricket,
With fever sharply singing,
My body charmed by itself alone
Listens, happily tingling.

A prisoner in soft and rustling chains
And manacles of living hay,
Sweetly defeated by the grass, partially
Buried by the great master's lay –

Docile earth and harsh, fermenting scents,
Inventing alcohol, worms, weeds and grain,
Ready to receive my slender frame
Like a long familiar refrain.

How much sacred beauty we waste to
Hide the painful mind from the world, where
It goes back to the dust at last, proud of being
Chased by a cricket here…

A Sign

With their forests like a
Nervous and trembling coat
Of fur, the hills still wait for
A sign from above or below;

With innocent eyes that
Marvel at a presentiment,
Deer still lurk in wait for
A subtle sign or hint;

And birds in flight,
And bats hanging blind,
Are ready to receive
The decisive sign.

Be patient, oh forests,
Blinded birds, be patient there,
And wait where you are,
You innocent deer.

I cannot leave,
I don't comprehend
The total meaning
Of this mistake, destined

To end with a sign that
I do not want to make:
Grant me one more summer, forests;
Show me mercy, hills and lakes.

There Are Some Mornings

There are some mornings when
The seed gods recognise me,
They look at me in wonder
And say,
It's like we've seen you before somewhere,
I have the same impression
But I don't remember where it was,
And not to disappoint them
I smile
And nod my head.

Wasn't it you
This spring
In the green darkness
Of that palace underground?
From time to time we heard clear
Footsteps ring...
And though I didn't recall
I murmured – yes, yes.

Yes, it must have been me,
I know you too,
Diminutive gods
Scattered on the earth and in the dew,
And even though I don't remember,
I feel like I, too, come
From a world
Where once I worshipped you.

A world in which
I had a purpose then
And where, some day,
I'll ask to be taken in.

Portrait with Cherry Earrings

Still ripening every day
Hanging from my ears
Today in pairs
Tomorrow gone away

Sweet berries
Childlike cherries
Just like before
Your shoulders are

Lithe and round
When you bend over
And once more count
The leaves of clover

Just like then
You still amaze
Me with sweet bouquets
Beneath the quince

You still gather fruit
Under trees in the sun
Sometimes peach sometimes plum
With your eyelids shut

Monday and Tuesday
Thursday and Friday
To bring me here
From my younger years

I wear these sleek
Ephemeral earrings
Of cherries surrounding
This dead cheek

And funereal
Wreaths of peonies
Braided with poppies
Strange on my skull.

BIBLIOGRAPHY

Taken together, the four volumes of Ana Blandiana's poetry published by Bloodaxe Books from 2014 to 2025 – all translated by Paul Scott Derrick and Viorica Patea – comprise her collected poems to date in English translation. These editions include complete translations of the respective collections as well as some uncollected poems and poems which have only appeared in selected volumes in Romanian. This listing shows which volume of translations covers each of her collections published in Romanian, all from Bucharest publishing houses.

* Selected volumes published in Romania are included only where these feature poems not published in her separate collections which have been translated and incorporated into the Bloodaxe editions.

2014   MNLA4   *My Native Land A4*
2017   SHES   *The Sun of Hereafter* • *Ebb of the Senses*
2021   FB   *Five Books*
2025   SW   *The Shadow of Words*

1964   *Persoana intâia plural* (First Person Plural), Editura pentru Literatură. SW.

1966   *Călcâiul vulnerabil* (Achilles' Heel), Editura Tineretului. SW

1969   *A treia taină* (The Third Sacrament), Editura pentru Literatură. SW.

1970* *Cinczeci de poeme* (Fifty Poems), Editions Eminescu. SW.

1972   *Octombrie, Noiembrie, Decembrie* (October, November, December), Cartea Românească. FB.

1974* *Poezi* (Poems), Editura Cartea Românească. SW.

1977   *Somnul din somn* (Sleep within Sleep), Cartea Românească. SW.

1981   *Ochiul de greier* (The Cricket's Eye), Editura Albatros. SW.

1985   *Stea de pradă* (Predator Star), Bucharest: Cartea Românească. FB.

1990   *Arhitectura valurilor* (The Architecture of Waves), Cartea
       Românească. FB.

2000   *Soarele de apoi* (The Sun of the Hereafter), Editura DU Style.
       SHES.

2004   *Refluxul sensurilor* (Ebb of the Senses), Humanitas. SHES.

2010   *Patria mea A4* (My Native Land A4), Humanitas. MNLA4.

2016   *Orologiul fără ore* (Clock without Hours), Humanitas. FB.

2018   *Variațiuni pe o temă dată* (Variations on a Given Theme),
       Humanitas. FB.

THE TRANSLATORS

Paul Scott Derrick and Viorica Patea are joint translators of four volumes by Ana Blandiana published by Bloodaxe Books: *My Native Land A4* (2014), *The Sun of Hereafter • Ebb of the Senses* (2017), *Five Books* (2021) and *The Shadow of Words* (2025). They also co-edited *Modernism Revisited: Transgressing Boundaries and Strategies of Renewal in American Poetry* (Rodopi, 2007).

Paul Scott Derrick is a Senior Lecturer (retired) in American literature at the University of Valencia. His critical works include *Thinking for a Change: Gravity's Rainbow and Symptoms of the Paradigm Shift in Occidental Culture* (1994), *We stand before the secret of the world: Traces along the Pathway of American Transcendentalism* (2003) and *Lines of Thought* (2015). He has edited and co-translated into Spanish a number of critical editions of works by Ralph Waldo Emerson, Emily Dickinson (Spanish and Catalan), and Sarah Orne Jewett. With Viorica Patea, he co-edited *Modernism Revisited* (Rodopi, 2007). He is also co-editor, with Norman Jope and Catherine E. Byfield, of *The Companion to Richard Berengarten* (Shearsman, 2016), and with Sean Rys, of *Managing The Manager: Critical Essays on Richard Berengarten's Book-length Poem* (Cambridge Scholars, 2019). With Miguel Teruel, he has published a translation of Berengarten's *Black Light* into Spanish (Luz Negra, JPM Ediciones, 2012). In addition, he has translated Enric Valor's *Rondalles Valencianes* (Valencian Folktales) from Valencian into English with co-translator Maria-Lluïsa Gea-Valor. These have been published serially by Routledge: *Valencian Folktales* (2023), *Valencian Folktales, Volume 2* (2024) and *Valencian Folktales, Volume 3* (2025).

Viorica Patea is Professor of American Literature at the University of Salamanca, where she teaches American and English literature. Her published books include studies on Sylvia Plath, Walt Whitman, Ezra Pound, and T.S. Eliot's *The Waste Land* (Cátedra, 2022). She has edited numerous collections of essays, such as *Critical Essays on the Myth of the American Adam* (Ediciones U. Salamanca, 2001), *Short*

Story Theories: A Twenty-First-Century Perspective (Rodopi, 2012, which received the 2013 Javier Coy Research Award for the best edited book from the Spanish Association of American Studies), and, together with Paul Scott Derrick, *Modernism Revisited: Transgressing Boundaries and Strategies of Renewal in American Poetry* (Rodopi, 2007). Recently she has co-edited with John Gery a bilingual anthology of poetry, '*Song Up Out of Spain': Poems in Tribute to Ezra Pound*, and a book of essays, *Ezra Pound & the Spanish World*, both published by Clemson University Press in 2023 and 2024. She has written extensively on Ana Blandiana's oeuvre, which she has also translated into Spanish: with Fernando Sánchez Miret two of Blandiana's short story books, *Proyectos de Pasado* and *Las Cuatro estaciones* (Periférica 2008, 201), and with Natalia Carbajosa, Blandiana's complete poems published by Pre-textos, Galaxia Gutenberg and Visor press. Her research interests include foremost poetry and poetics, as well as comparative studies in witness literature of East-European countries. She is currently working on a book project on Pound's later *Cantos*.